Anonymous

Illustrated History Of Salem & Environs

Anonymous

Illustrated History Of Salem & Environs

ISBN/EAN: 9783337820534

Printed in Europe, USA, Canada, Australia, Japan

Cover: Foto ©ninafisch / pixelio.de

More available books at **www.hansebooks.com**

Illustrated History

of

Salem and Environs

Issued as the

Souvenir Edition

of the

SALEM EVENING NEWS

and

Describing and Illustrating Salem, Massachusetts and
Immediate Vicinity from First Settlement
to Present Day.

Compiled by C. B. Gillespie.

Containing:

Concise History; Old Landmarks; Present and Former Residents; its Institutions, Buildings, Beauty of Scenery; Comfortable Homes; Portraits and Biographical Sketches of Active Men, also those noted in Public, Business and Professional Life; its Manufacturing and Trade; Statements of Resources and Advantages of Locality; its Health, Wealth, Prosperity and Future Possibilities.

Introduction.

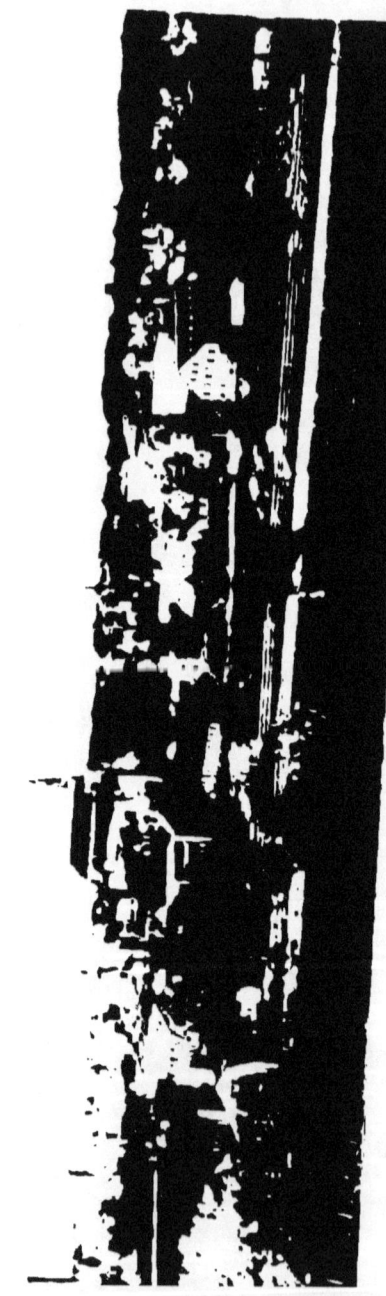

A PARTIAL BIRD'S EYE VIEW OF SALEM

1626... Salem ...1897

PERHAPS greater difficulties would encounter a narrator of the history of Salem than would be met by a writer attempting to give a complete sketch of any city of its size in New England. This would not be, however, from any lack of material, but from the wealth of historic dleton, Wenham, Peabody and portions of Topsfield and Lynn. Had not Salem's generosity prompted her to part with her early territorial possessions she would be today a city of 100,000 instead of 35,000 population. Salem, however, from its convenient location, regains much in

COUNTY COURT HOUSES, SALEM

events which have made Salem noted the world over.

By virtue of its having been settled in 1626, Salem is four years older than Boston. Fate prescribed that Salem should part with a large portion of her territory. The original township included Beverly, Danvers, Manchester, Marblehead, Mid- the way of business, evidenced conclusively by its numerous large and prosperous mercantile establishments, educational institutions and otherwise. In reality, while Salem in her own name is in possession of less than forty thousand inhabitants, the volume of trade is as large as in an ordinary locality of 80,000 population. Salem, by virtue of its settlement, holds the distinction of being the second oldest town in New England, and history decreed her to be the second in Massachusetts to become an incorporated city. The city charter was granted March 15, 1836.

In its very early history Salem incurred the name of the City of Witches, which sobriquet will doubtless be borne by her to eternity. Although innocent people were hanged on Gallows Hill, and many were caused to flee from Salem for their lives on account of the witchcraft delusion, it should be remembered that this superstition was prevalent the world over justice to Salem it should also be remembered that the jail delivery, which took place after nineteen persons had been hanged, sixteen of whom were women, and Giles Corey, who would not plead, was crushed to death, was the commencement of the breaking up of the unfortunate and execrable delusion which had existed the world over for several years. It was at the house of Rev. Samuel Parris, pastor of the Salem village church, that the beginning of the persecution here of supposed witches found its inception. That the actions of the victims, afterwards executed, and the causes as to the accusations, were innocent, is not questioned at

SALEM AND BEVERLY BRIDGE

at that time. In this enlightened age careful readers of history do not credit Salem as being responsible for the acts of the deluded people, who, by acting under their honest convictions, caused the death of innocent persons, giving the city the name it is now forced to bear. In this unfortunate eventful period of the history of Salem, it should be remembered that the judges who presided at the several trials of persons accused and subsequently executed for witchcraft, held here, were acting under English rule, and that but a small majority of those participating in the trials were actually Salem people. In the present day, but like many harmless acts these were productive of great trouble by misapprehension on the part of the people of early days—witchcraft having been firmly believed in for several hundred years previous to the landing of the Pilgrims, in the old world. Authorities differ as to the facts concerning witchcraft delusion here. "The History of Salem Witchcraft," by Nevins, 1892, is generally accepted as authoritative. According to his research, Rev. Samuel Parris had a woman servant named Tituba, born in the West Indies, who was more or less familiar with the tricks and

SALEM 1626-1897

juggling practiced by semi-civilized races, similar to that to which she belonged. It is taken for granted that this woman exhibited these tricks to Mr. Parris's daughter and niece, who described them to their young friends. Their companions becoming interested and astonished at the wonderful acts of contortion and juggling, they afterwards frequently requested the servant to repeat them. It being the nature of the young to imitate, they soon tried to astonish their neighbors by going through the peculiar actions, uttering strange cries, and making mysterious signs. The effect on the staid and rigidly strict elder people caused by their unnatural demeanor was such that they demanded an explanation and quoting Mr. Nevins words "The girls probably realized that if the exact truth were known to their elders they would be severely punished — possibly publicly disciplined in church. To prevent this may they not have claimed that they could not help doing as they did? They undoubtedly had some knowledge of witchcraft; enough at least to enable them to make a pretence of being bewitched. The girls could not for a moment realize the terrible consequences which were to follow. Having taken the first step they were in the position of all who take the first step in falsehood or any wrong doing,— another step became necessary, and then another. At all events, they accused Tituba, Sarah Good, 'a melancholy distracted person,' and Sarah Osburn, 'a bed-ridden old woman,' with having bewitched them." The accused women were arrested February 29, 1692, and the next day the examination of their cases was begun in Salem, and resulted so unfavorably that all of them were sent to jail in Boston, March 7th. Sarah Good was hanged July 16, 1692; Sarah Osburn died in prison, and Tituba was never tried before any court, but was sold to pay her prison fees (she being a slave), after lying in prison thirteen months. Although Sarah Good was one of the first three arrested on a charge of witchcraft, the first one to be executed as a witch in Salem was Bridget Bishop, who was arrested April 19, 1692, and hanged June 10th. Her death warrant is the only one that was

SECTION OF SUMMER STREET, SALEM.

kept, and it is now framed and hangs in office of the clerk of the courts at Salem. Very many arrests were made, and for a time it seemed as if the delusion were destined to continue for years and to cause the execution of scores of Salem people, but its departure was almost as sudden as its arrival, and Salem was one of the first New England towns to recognize its folly. Among those accused was a man, Giles Corey, who refused to plead because he felt that the court was so constituted that if he pleaded not guilty he would surely be condemned, and although he knew that a plea of guilty would save his life he would not swear falsely in order to escape a death sentence. The old English law provided that one who refused to plead would be pressed until a plea was made or life destroyed, and therefore Corey was bound and placed prostrate on the earth; and great rocks were heaped upon his chest until he could hardly breathe. He not only refused to plead but told the officers to increase the weight, for death was the only way to end the matter, as he would never say guilty or not guilty. And thus he perished. On a bronze tablet near the corner of Washington and Lynde streets may be found a record of Corey's execution and also other features of the witchcraft period. It reads as follows: "Nearly opposite this spot stood, in the middle of the street, a building devoted from 1677 until 1718 to municipal and judicial uses. In it in 1692 were tried and condemned for witchcraft most of the nineteen persons who suffered death on the gallows. Giles Corey was here put to trial on the same charge, and, refusing to plead was taken away and pressed to death. In January, 1693, twenty-one persons were tried here for witchcraft, of whom eighteen were acquitted and three condemned, but later set free, together with about 150 accused persons in the general delivery at the jail in May, 1693, previously alluded to."

While Salem is forced to bear an unsavory reputation on account of the witchcraft delusion by no means wholly deserved, but which, nevertheless brings many visitors yearly within its borders, its historic spots are numerous and the deeds of residents from its early foundation have made the city famous the world over. Before the revolution Salem people were prompt and determined in their opposition to British tyranny, shown more conclusively after the landing of British troops; and to her credit be it said that her firm and bold stand was the cause of the first blood shed in the revolution in a combat with regular soldiers. Salem people through representatives took a prominent part in causing the repeal of the Stamp Act, and the repeal of that act, which formed so important an event in the pages of American history, caused the greatest rejoicing here. The people of this locality were no less determined in their opposition to subsequent attempts to tax them beyond reason. The early business men of Salem showed their independence in 1768, when they agreed not to send any further orders for goods, and from January 1, 1769 to January 1, 1770, not to import nor to purchase of others any kind of merchandise from Great Britain, except coal, salt and some other articles necessary to carry on the fishery."

In a historical sketch of Salem, written

SECTION OF CHESTNUT STREET, SALEM

by H. M. Batchelder and Charles S. Osgood, "An Historical Sketch of Salem, 1626 - 1879" it is said: "It was the fortune of Salem to be the theatre of the opening scenes in the great struggle that was to end in the independence of the colonies. There is no other year in the annals of Salem so memorable and crowded so full of historic events, as the year which began on the first day of June, 1774. Here during that time, were convened the last Provincial Assembly and First Provincial Congress;" here were chosen the first delegates to the Continental congress ; here the assembled province first formally renounced allegiance to the Imperial Legislature : here was made the first attempt to enforce the last oppressive acts of parliament, and here that attempt was resisted ; and here, though no mortal wound was given, was shed the first blood of the American Revolution. The good people of Salem were naturally strenuously opposed to a second war with England as they were at that time extensively interested in shipping, their vessels being sent to all parts of the world, making Salem famous in foreign commerce. Yet when war was actually declared, and notwithstanding that it meant a greater loss to the people here than elsewhere, the town main-

GALLOWS HILL.   OLD SHATTUCK HOUSE.

tained throughout the War of 1812 an enviable reputation for patriotism and bravery of its men in the bloody struggle for supremacy. In this Salem sustained and added to her good record gained during the Revolution and strongly supported the government in the conflict which at first seemed almost hopeless to the United States. The deeds of valor of Salem privateers caused them to become both dreaded and hated by Great Britain, for many an English vessel was captured through the vigilance of these privateers and the work accomplished by them was a great blow to English commerce. Many of these conflicts on the high seas were

A GROUP OF SALEM CHURCHES OF THE PRESENT DAY

from the close of the Revolution to the Embargo Act in 1808 proved the brightest period in her commercial prosperity, Salem being far more important than Boston, in this respect, in former years. Two governors of the Commonwealth of Massachusetts made Salem their place of residence, namely:—William Endicott, who filled the office of chief executive for sixteen years, and Bradstreet, the nestor governor, who came here with Winthrop in June, 1630. The latter outlived the whole Winthrop party and died in Salem, in 1697. He was twice governor of Massachusetts and filled all the important offices, first from 1679 to 1686, when the State Charter was annulled, and later from 1689 to 1692. Gov. Bradstreet headed a Revolutionary movement in prisoning Andros and snatching away his sword which three years later he delivered to Sir William Phipps, at that time governor under the new charter granted by William III and becoming his first assistant at the remarkable age of eighty nine. Salem has twice been the seat of government,—first under Endicott in 1628-9 and later under Gage in 1774. From 1800 to 1810 the population of Salem increased from 9,457 to 12,617. Salem's importance as a great commercial center was recognized the world over in the early history of the town; and her record is that of the pioneer in the India trade. In looking at such cities as New York and Philadelphia of today and realizing their importance in the transaction of commerce with Eastern ports it would indeed be hard to realize that Salem was once many times greater, and still more surprising to know that the names of those sea-ports were not recognized, while that of Salem was universally known. Such, however, was the case as in her early history she was supposed to be the greatest of American cities. In the early part of the nineteenth century, it is stated upon good authority that there were 198 vessels owned in Salem and her ships are known to have been the first to carry the American flag and open trade with St. Petersburg, Zanzibar, Sumatra, Calcutta, Bombay, Batavia, Arabia, Madagascar and Australia. Salem is not only noted for its former importance from the commercial standpoint, for its historic places are not only numerous but bring to mind many events of interest to the entire United States. Perhaps Salem can boast of more noted men among her early residents than any city of its population in America. Hence the city is dotted with old historic residences and buildings. The Roger Williams House is situated at the corner of Essex and North streets. This was owned in 1635-6 by Roger Williams who resided in Salem and was the teacher at the First Church of Salem for a few months in 1631 and again in 1633 and 1634-5 was minister of the church. He was much sought after by Salem people as both teacher and

BIG ELM TREE. BOSTON STREET.

SALEM 1626-1807

A GROUP OF FAMOUS SALEM MEN

pastor. The general court at Boston, however, unseated Salem deputies for the efforts of their constituents in retaining him and finally magistrates sent a vessel to Salem in which to remove him to England. The story of his escape from their clutches, flight and subsequent founding of Rhode Island, is well known to the readers of American history. He was of course a man whose good example was of profit to the people of his day and one whose independence of thought tended to enlighten this country and the world. He was a close friend of Gov. Endicott and a confidential advisor as well, and those who were fearful of the result when Governor Endicott cut the cross from the flag of Great Britain attributed the act to William's influence. The Williams house is known also as the old Witch House from the tradition existing relative to the preliminary hearings supposed to have been held under its roof of several accused of witchcraft. The house is still standing, but has been materially changed in appearance. The house is also known as the oldest house in Salem and vicinity and many thousand visitors yearly are attracted to it. Salem is also the birth place of Timothy Pickering

SALEM PUBLIC LIBRARY.

who won marked distinction in the Revolutionary War. He was known as a stout leader of the patriots and was an adjutant general in the American Army. He figured conspicuously at the Battles of Germantown and Brandywine. He also was among those who made the brave stand in holding the North End

tary of war and secretary of state. Nathaniel Bowditch, the translator of La Place (the desk on which he did the work is now at the Essex Institute), was also born in Salem, March 26, 1773. In the same house Rev. Samuel Johnson, a talented liberal preacher and author of several works on Oriental religions, was

ESSEX COUNTY COURT HOUSES AND INTERIOR LAW LIBRARY

at a very critical time during an important contest in Salem. He afterwards became noted as a statesman, becoming representative, senator and later a member of Washington's cabinet, by whom he was appointed and under whom he held the offices of postmaster general, secre-

also born. Harrison Gray Otis, an eminent scholar, orator, author and statesman resided here and moved here to office. He served in the British Army during the Revolution and afterwards wrote a history of Boston entitled Count Rumford Island, a monograph on chief of the Batavian Army. The historian and author William Hickling Prescott, D. C. L., who wrote "Conquest of Mexico," "Ferdinand and Isabella," and "Philip Second" was born in a house on the site of which now stands Plummer Hall. The house in which this noted author first saw light of day was built by Nathan Reed. He

professor of mathematics at Harvard College, was born on Warren street. He was one of the most noted mathematicians of his time. He became the head of the United States Coast Survey and made a change in the standard time of the continent, establishing the meridians which have since regulated and controlled

MILES WARD AND JACOB CROWNINSHIELD HOUSE.   CABOT AND JUDGE ENDICOTT HOUSE.

studied medicine with Dr. Holyoke, and conducted an iron works at Danversport, and as far back as 1789 tested the steamboat in the Danvers and North Rivers. Among his passengers on the first trial trip were Gov. John Hancock, Nathan Dane, Rev. Prince, D.D., and Dr. Holyoke. Benjamin Pierce, at one time

the "time of day." A noted Greek lexicographer was John Pickering, L. L. D. He was born in Salem in 1777, lived on Chestnut street and was a son of Col. Timothy Pickering. The noted compiler of Worcester's dictionary, Joseph E. Worcester, at one time taught school here. He had among his pupils Nathaniel Hawthorne William Wetmore Story, the noted sculptor and author, was born in Salem in a brick house on Winter street, which was built by Judge Joseph Story. General Lafayette was entertained at this house. Rufus Choate, the able orator and advocate, once lived on Lynde street in Salem. Benjamin Goodhue, a member in a handsome brick mansion in Washington square, and at his house Daniel Webster, Henry Clay and many other noted men were guests. The greatest merchant and ship owner of his time in the United States, William Gray, came to Salem at an early age. He became Lieutenant Governor of the state and

PEABODY ACADEMY OF SCIENCE

of the United States Senate from Massachusetts from 1796 to 1800, was born September 20, 1748. He occupied a house on Essex street. United States Senator Nathaniel Silsbee, a member of the U. S. Senate from 1826 to 1835, was born in Salem in a house on Daniels street. He afterwards built and resided held the office during 1810 etc. He lived at one time in the house which was in 1800 converted into the Sun Tavern, the old sign of which is preserved by the Danvers Historical Society. The house was afterwards called the Essex Coffee House, and is remembered as such by older residents. Benjamin W. Crownin-

SALEM 1626-1897

shield, a member of congress, United
States senator and secretary of the navy
during President Madison's administration from 1814 to 1818, resided in a mansion which he built on Derby street, which
is now converted into the Old Ladies'
Home. At his house President Monroe
dined and both commodores Perry and
Bainbridge were guests.
The secretary of war in
President Cleveland's cabinet, William C. Endicott,
who was formerly a judge of
the supreme court of Mas-
sachusetts, resided for thirty
years on Essex street in the
old colonial residence, a
house built by Joseph Cabot
in 1748. Judge Endicott
was born in the Crownin-
shield house on Derby street.
To the many historical spots
referred to briefly in the
foregoing, large time honored stores be attracted ann-

Salem of Today

Is seventeen miles from Boston and is the
recognized political centre of Essex county,
being a shire town and the seat of the
principal county offices. The state census
of 1895 gave a population of 34,473, representing 7,263 families. This was an in-

crease of nearly
4,000 over the
last enu-
meration tak-
en five years prev-
iously. Upon
estimate popu-
lation of Salem
at the present
time is 35,000.
The assessed
polls number
9,560, and the
voting strength
is 5,903. An
estimate of 6,100. The latest assessors' figures
give a total valuation of $25,971,200, the
tax rate being $17.50 per thousand. The
area of the city is about 4,000 acres.

GENERAL.

As a matter of permanent abode, Salem
affords every convenience of existing

AMONG THE BREAKERS AT BAKER'S ISLAND.

ally, particularly in the summer months,
when there are frequent pilgrimages to
Salem from all parts of the country. In
the midst of the activities of the present,
numerous organizations keep fresh the
memory of the former days and generations, from which so much of interest and
real worth may be gained.

city, the pure atmosphere of the country and the delights of a sea shore resort. A large element in the population is engaged in Boston during the day, retaining a home in Salem. With the more conservative feeling which nearly always may be found in such historical localities as this, is mingled the leaven of the younger and more active business leaders of the city. For the transient, there are good and abundant hotel facilities. The regular sessions of the superior and supreme courts held in Salem attract an unusually able legal talent, both …

located on Washington street, near Essex.

RELIGIOUS.

To the early settlers of Salem, religious observances were meat and drink, and in view of the prominence in history of incidents connected with the same, a glance at the status of the various denominations in the city will not be without interest. … Unitarian bodies in the … the East Church … in 1629, now acts … the … Episcopal soon …

WASHINGTON STREET, LOOKING NORTH.

professional men resident in the city take high rank.

ALDERMEN.

The law-making power is vested … mayor and board … several aldermen elected annually at large, at present four members being elected at large, one each of the six wards. Each board chooses a chairman from its own membership. The policy of the city … late years has generally been adverse to the licensed sale of intoxicating liquor. The city had, of stone and brick and … ceremonies at …

Roman Catholic, three each, Episcopal and Methodist Episcopal, two each, and one each of Adventist, Dead Mates of Evangelicals, Friends, New Jerusalem, Universalist, Christian Science, Spiritualist, … Jewish … congregation. There are also numerous efforts in the line of mission work, Y. M. C. A., etc. Many of the church buildings exceed in size architectural attractiveness, and the … given except in a select body of men. A fine structure for the use of the Y. M. C. A. is now being erected. The general interest in this work is deep and the support generous and sincere.

EDUCATIONAL.

A national fame is enjoyed by the schools of Salem; in every department the best is demanded. School affairs are administered by a board of three members from each ward, elected for three years, the terms of one third of the board expiring each year. The mayor and president of the common council are members ex officio, the former acting as chairman. A president and secretary are also elected. The executive officer is the superintendent. The teaching force numbers 127, not including special instructors, as of music and of drawing. The classical and high school is located on Broad street. There are five grammar, thirteen primary and five kindergarten schools, besides an industrial school and several rooms in the state normal school building used as model schools. As recommended by the principal of the normal school, the teachers in these rooms are elected by the school board. The larger part of the teachers now employed are graduates of the normal school. The latest figures give the total enrollment of pupils as 4,525, with about 2,000 in parochial schools, of which there are three in the city. Salem is largely represented in the higher institutions of learning scattered throughout the country, and the efficiency of the preparation for advanced studies therein is found to be most complete. The city annually appropriates more than $100,000 for school purposes.

FINANCIAL.

There are seven national banks in the city—Asiatic, First, Mercantile, Merchants, National Exchange, Naumkeag and Salem—with a combined capital of $2,015,000 and abundant surplus. Over 31,000 depositors appear on the books of the Salem and the Salem Five Cents Savings banks. Two co-operative banks, the Roger Conant and the Salem, largely designed to assist laboring people to the ownership of homes, have been doing a most substantial work for some years. The Essex Mutual, Holyoke Mutual, Salem Mutual and Salem Marine Insurance companies have their headquarters in this city and are represented in many other cities and towns. The greatest insurance concerns in this and other countries have agencies here. The management of these great financial interests is a happy medium between conservatism and progressiveness, and by long and successful careers has gained the confidence of all.

MANUFACTURING.

In the way of manufacturing, Salem is pre-eminently a leather city. From the most modest beginnings, this business has enormously increased and the aggregate output involves millions of dollars annually. The product is varied, but of an extra quality throughout. Over 1,000 men are employed in this industry alone. Closely allied to this is the shoe and findings manufacturing, some twenty-five firms

ESSEX STREET, NEAR PUBLIC LIBRARY.

SALEM 1626-1897

SALEM HOSPITAL CHARTER STREET

being so engaged. This product is shipped largely to the south and west. The textile interests are extensive, the annual production of cotton cloth exceeding 15,000,000 yards. Other important industries are the manufacture of bagging, rosin, paints, dyes, bicycles and chemicals and the preparing of leads, oils, etc. In the city are located car works, foundries, machine shops, wood and marble working establishments. Every inducement can be offered for manufacturing concerns to locate in Salem, and the list of those availing themselves of these advantages is a lengthy one. The city escaped the recent extended commercial depression with comparatively small damage, and the relations of employed with employer are generally amicable.

MARITIME

To those familiar with the stories of the decline of Salem's water commerce, it may come as somewhat of a surprise to learn that in regard to tonnage of arrivals, the traffic was never so great as for the last fiscal year, when the 1902 arrivals represented an aggregate tonnage of 508,839. To be sure, vessels do not bear to this port the wealth of the orient, but immense coal concerns have stations in the city from which their staple is distributed over a wide area. This is brought entirely by water, amounting last year to 411,000 tons. Many manufactories receive their coal supply direct from vessel to engine room. From the British provinces, practically the only foreign parts from which there are now arrivals; coal and lumber are received in large quantities. In the ports of Salem and Beverly, the territory covered by the Salem district, fifty-five vessels are owned, with a tonnage of 4,116. The custom house is located on Derby street and is of historical interest through the writings of Nathaniel Hawthorne.

RETAIL BUSINESS.

Salem is the great shopping mart of this portion of the county. The retail business is grouped largely on Washington and Essex streets, the latter thoroughfare being a veritable Strand. The varied stocks are complete and up-to-date and the market truly metropolitan. In that feature of nineteenth-century retail trade, the department store, Salem is not lacking. A Board of Trade has been in existence since 1889.

ESSEX STREET, NEAR HAMILTON.

TRANSPORTATION AND COMMUNICATION.

The transportation facilities are largely in the hands of the Boston & Maine and the Lynn & Boston roads, both systems being given more extended notice elsewhere in this volume. During the summer season, excursion steamers run to Boston and Baker's island. The Western Union and Postal companies furnish telegraphic and cable service to all the world. Salem is remembered as the home of Prof. Bell at the time of the announcement of his triumph with the telephone, and the system of today is the best obtainable. Branch offices are maintained at Peabody and Beverly in connection with the central exchange of the New England Telephone and Telegraph Company, the 425 instruments being scattered throughout the cities of Salem and Beverly and the towns of Boxford, Danvers, Essex, Hamilton, Ipswich, Lynnfield, Manchester, Marblehead, Middleton, Peabody, Topsfield and Wenham. Besides this immense local business, trunk lines allow of communication with all important points in New England, Canada and the states east of the Mississippi river. Collections and distribution of mails are frequent within the prescribed limits and the mail schedule in all directions is unusually complete. The American, Lakeman, Merritt, Moulton, Savory, Cogswell and Marston expresses, with a large number of local and suburban carriers, do a general transportation business.

PUBLIC IMPROVEMENTS.

Gas and electricity in abundance are at the command of the citizens of Salem for lighting purposes, both the Salem Gas Light company and the Salem Electric Lighting company doing a large and successful business. Electricity is almost exclusively used for street lighting, the arc and incandescent lamps numbering 104 and 616 respectively, and burn all and every night during the year. The principal source of the water supply is Wenham Lake, having an area of 251 acres, Longham brook affords an additional supply, the 20,000,000 gallon reservoir being located at North Beverly. The distribution of this abundant supply is as complete as could well be the case, water takers numbering over 10,000. The purity and security of the water system is guarded thoroughly and the supply will rank with the best for general quality. The streets are cared for by trained employees, the accepted ways aggregating seventy five miles, of which an unusually large proportion are paved or macadamized. The annual appropriation for this department is in the vicinity of $60,000. A comprehensive sewerage plan is now in contemplation, making use of the North river. Sewerage is now emptied into the stream before mentioned and into the sea. A park commission of five members cares for the public breathing places, of which the Willows, a delightful resort on the harbor side, is the chief. The other tracts in charge of the commission are the Common at Washington square, Ledge Hill Park, otherwise known as the Mack farm, Liberty Hill and Rowell's Field. In the course of Nature, resting places for the dead must be set apart, the leading burial spots of the city being Harmony Grove and Greenlawn, of great natural beauty and under careful supervision. The other cemeteries are St. Mary's (Catholic), Friends', Howard Street, Broad Street and Charter Street.

CITY HALL, WASHINGTON STREET.

the latter the oldest in the city and containing many graves of particular interest. At Greenlawn is the beautiful Dickson Memorial chapel. A board of health of five members keeps a constant vigil for the weal of the inhabitants of the city; epidemics are unknown and the death rate is low. At Salem Neck, upon the almshouse grounds, is a small hospital under the care of the board, to be used in cases of threatened contagion. The Salem Hospital, located on Charter street, was organized from a fund contributed by Capt. John Bertram and other citizens. The hospital is managed by a private company, but admission is open to all worthy persons. A training school for nurses is in connection.

HISTORICAL, LITERARY AND SOCIAL INSTITUTIONS, ETC.

Of the work of the Essex Institute, extended reference is made elsewhere in this volume. At the East India Marine hall, 161 Essex street, are the valuable collections of the Peabody Academy of Science. The trustees organized in 1868, having received funds by gift from George Peabody of London. With the museum of the East India Marine Society and the natural history collections of the Essex Institute as a nucleus, many additions have been made until the collections are a marvel of completeness. The three kingdoms of the natural world, particularly as found in this county, may here be studied thoroughly. There are also historical collections of objects representing various phases of life among the eastern nations and much of value to those interested in the early marine history of Salem. The museum is free to all. The East India Marine Society is still in existence and does a large amount of charitable work. Salem is a centre for the work of the American Association for the Advancement of Science. In the Salem public library are over 33,000 volumes and in the libraries of the Salem Athenaeum and the Salem Fraternity, 24,500 and 4,221 volumes respectively. The latter furnishes evening instruction and amusement designed more particularly for working people. For members of the Salem Charitable Mechanic Association, 6,000 volumes are at command. In the way of secret fraternities, the various degrees of Masonry and Odd Fellowship are liberally represented. Other orders are the American Legion of Honor, A. O. U. W., O. U. A. M., D. of L., G. A. R., S. of V., Red Men, K. of C., K. of H., K. of P., Good Fellows, Forresters, N. E. O. P., Pilgrim Fathers, Royal Arcanum, U. O. G. C. and I. O. L. A. Social clubs number over twenty-five, of which the Salem, Colonial and Thorndike clubs are chief, with numerous musical, labor, veteran firemen, legal, medical, press, temperance, political, military, boating, athletic, marine and school organizations. The city has not, as yet, a first-class amusement place, but Mechanic,

EAST INDIA MARINE HALL, ESSEX STREET.

Cadet and Academy halls furnish abundant opportunities for assemblages of all kinds.

CHARITABLE AND REFORMATORY.

Twenty funds, ranging in amount from $500 to $40,000, are held in trust by the city government, the incomes being used in the supplying of food, fuel, etc., to the worthy poor. The Association for the Relief of Aged and Destitute Women in Salem has been carrying on its beneficent work for nearly forty years and the Bertram Home for Aged Men, located on Derby street, has been incorporated since 1877. The Old Ladies' Home is upon the same street. The City Orphan Asylum of Salem, Lafayette street, is a Roman Catholic institution, in charge of Sisters of Charity. On Winter island is the Plummer Farm School of Reform for Boys. The original bequest of Miss Caroline Plummer has been added to and the school is now generously endowed. Incorrigible truancy is punished here. The Seaman's Orphan and Children's Friend Society, organized in 1830, provides a home on Carpenter street for orphan and needy children. The Woman's Friend Society and Working Women's Bureau has a home on Essex street. The Salem Female Charitable Society and the Seaman's Widow and Orphan Association are old organizations. Frequent conferences of the Relief Committee and the Associated Charities are held. The charitable work done in connection with the various religious and social bodies reaches large proportions.

POLICE.

The police force of the city is under the direction of a marshal, assistant marshal, captain and sergeant. The patrol consists of seven day and twenty four night men, placed in the business and residential sections to the best possible advantage, and a substitute force may be drawn upon in cases of necessity. Two janitors and a driver are also in service. The headquarters are at 11 Front street. Two signal systems are used - the Metropolitan and the Pierce & Jones. The boxes of both, numbering over eighty, may be used for both police and fire signals, the alarms being repeated from the station all over the city, which requires constant attendance in the signal room. Although the tenure of the entire department is upon an annual basis, changes are very few, the services of the officers and the major portion of the patrol extending over a period of years. The able and unbiased work for which the force is noted has its reward in continued incumbency of office. A relief association has been doing a most helpful work for years, nearly every member of the department being connected with the same. Most liberal sums are paid in cases of disability or death. Criminal cases have their inception in the First Essex District

THE FIRST MEETING HOUSE.

court, held at 193 Washington street.

FIRE DEPARTMENT.

The term of the chief of this department is for three years and he is allowed two assistants. There are now in commission three steamers, each having a hose company attached, two unattached hose companies, one city and one aerial truck, one chemical engine, coal wagon, etc. The permanent force numbers sixteen, with ninety-one men on call. The system of inspection of buildings, electric wires, etc., is careful and thorough. Every effort for the prevention of destructive fires is made, with what success the relatively small annual losses give eloquent testimony. A firemen's relief association is incorporated.

IN RETROSPECT.

The foregoing pages touch upon the salient features of the great mass of material which presents itself to mind when one considers every-day life in Salem as affecting the citizenship at large. From the storied past, noble examples have been handed down and the lessons are not in vain, for the city of today has an existence in name and in fact, destined to place her in no mean position among the sister municipalities. In the golden age of national progress now about to dawn, New Salem by the sea will make good accounting of the abundant talents committed to her care. A perusal of the following pages would seem to indicate present prosperity.

Salem Board of Trade.

The first recorded meeting of the Salem Board of Trade was held on the evening of April 18, 1889, at the Essex house. The list of officers, as arranged at preliminary meetings, was announced as follows: President, E. Frank Balch; vice presidents, Thomas H. Johnson, Benjamin W. Russell, James F. Almy; treasurer, Charles F. Curwen; secretary, Edward F. Brown; executive committee, E. Frank Balch, C. F. Curwen, Henry W. Peabody, William M. Hill, J. W. Balcomb, George W. Williams, T. Frank Hunt, N. A. Horton, Frank Cousins, Z. A. Gallup, L. E. Millea, Henry A. Hale, George E. Pearson, Benjamin W. Russell, Thomas H. Johnson. Appropriate committees were then appointed and have since been maintained upon such departments

HOUSE OF SEVEN GABLES, TURNER STREET.

as finance, insurance, railroads and transportation, hospitality, new enterprises, rooms, etc. During its existence the board has had six presidents—E. Frank Balch, James F. Almy, Frank Cousins, E. A. Mackintire, C. A. Jordan, and the present incumbent, Paul B. Patten. The membership list lengthened rapidly and soon included by far the greater portion of the representative business leaders of the city. Rooms were engaged in the Hale block, Essex street, remaining here until the spring of 1897, when a removal was made to the building of the Master Builders' Association on Central street. From the first, Edward F. Brown has acted as secretary. The regular meeting night is the third Thursday of each month. Since 1889 the board has been no inconsiderable factor in the growth and development of the city, the good accomplished being much more than is apparent at the first glance. The individual and general business interests of the city have been advanced and a vast amount of information diffused as to the commercial advantages of Salem. The board early directed its attention to the matter of a water line to Boston, something of which the city had been devoid for several years, and its influence was potent in bringing about the present arrangements for water communication with the Hub during a large part of the year. In the matter of street transportation, vast improvements were brought about, even under the old horse car system. The present very acceptable transfer privileges are largely due to the agitation and interest of the Board of Trade. Within a few years the citizens of the city were obliged to resort to the railroad station for the purpose of commercial and social communication by telegraph. A committee of business men was chosen to confer with the Western Union management and the present convenient and commodious office on Washington street, near the business centre, is the result. The board has always worked in sympathy with and has been ably supported by the city governments during its history. This has resulted in many improvements about the city, notably the widening of Lafayette street. The foresight of the board in looking beyond the immediate matter of dollars and cents has been abundantly and repeatedly proven in this and kindred cases, by increased valuations and general improvement of property in the vicinity. All who are acquainted with Salem affairs for the last few years will call to mind several industries of greater or less magnitude which have located here and are now doing a substantial business, largely through the influence and alertness of this body. Sifting the wheat from the chaff, all schemes which upon investigation demanded unhealthy propping, have been set aside, the practical business men of the city realizing the value of self help to a reasonable degree and a legitimate competition. When a leading industry threatened removal, the board applied itself to the work of laboring with the managers with a view to a continuance here. To what extent this influence counted is perhaps not for outsiders to say, but certain it is that the enterprise was dissuaded from removal and still continues in its enlarged sphere of helpfulness and success in Salem. The matter of a thorough and reliable hydrographical survey in this vicinity under governmental auspices

E. F. BROWN, SEC'Y SALEM BOARD OF TRADE.

was thoroughly considered and a constant agitation kept up along this line. The late Gen. Cogswell re-enforced the work of the board and upon one occasion spoke upon the subject with great acceptance. Two liberal appropriations were secured from congress — one to provide for the survey and another for a dredging of the harbor. From time to time public functions have been held, with addresses by leading business and professional men upon such subjects as insurance, Alaska and its untold wealth, etc. A notable date in the board's history is Feb. 15, 1894, when a banquet was held at Hamilton hall, graced by the presence of Gov. Greenhalge, Speaker Meyer, Mayor Turner, and the representatives of similar organizations throughout the state. Many resolutions have been passed, declaring the sentiment of the board upon vital questions affecting the commercial interests of this section, including the reported discrimination against Boston in the matter of freight rates, bankruptcy legislation, better highways and improved railway communication with the cities of northern Essex county. The moral effect of these declarations, voicing the sentiment of the combined business elements of the city, could not but have been most salutary. The present board of officers is as follows: President, Paul B. Patten; vice presidents, W. G. Webber, T. F. Mack, J. Frank Dalton; treasurer, Charles W. Read; secretary, Edward F. Brown; directors, C. A. Jordan, Frank Cousins, W. A. Swan, S. H. Wilkins, Charles B. Balcomb, A. L. Huntington, Harry A. Whitehead, F. A. Wendell, E. H. Morse, George W. Pitman, W. K. Bigelow, J. W. Balcomb, E. A. Mackintire, W. S. Nichols, Jr., William Briggs. With such an officiary, the citizens of Salem may reasonably expect a continuance of the good work in behalf of the most substantial interests of the community.

Paul B. Patten.

The president of the Salem Board of Trade for 1897, was born in West Newbury, Mass., in 1837, and has been an active and interested resident of Salem for the past thirty-nine years. He attended the district school in his native town, and at the age of eleven went on a farm, where he gained a rugged physique. After two years he went to Merrimac and commenced to learn the trade of a blacksmith. His employers afterwards moved to Lynn, where he finished and became proficient at his trade. In 1859 he came to Salem, entering the shop of Abner C. Goodell, Sr., who conducted a blacksmithing and machinist shop. He continued in his employ and in that of the firm, the members of which were changed, during the next fourteen years. He then formed a partnership with Zina Goodell, and carried on the blacksmith and machinist business with him for nine years, at the end of which time he bought the business at the corner of Dodge and

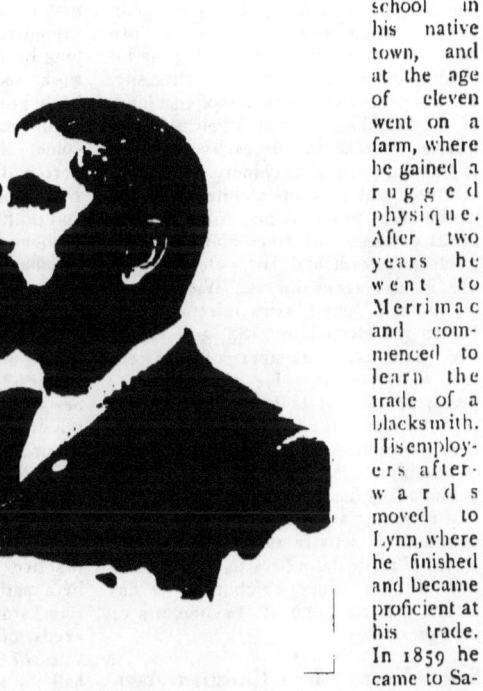

PAUL B. PATTEN, PRES. SALEM BOARD OF TRADE.

Lafayette streets. Some fourteen years ago he removed to his present works on Lafayette street, where his facilities were greatly increased. Mr. Patten is known by reputation to great extent throughout New England, a feature of his operations being the building of fire escapes. Many buildings throughout this state have been fitted with fire escapes by him, as well as many hotels at the White Mountains, notable among which is the Fabyan house. Mr. Patten is possessed of mechanical ingenuity and versatility, necessary qualifications of a successful man at his business, the variety of work coming to his establishment being of great diversity. He has perfected a number of machines of different kinds and is rarely, if ever, unable to make the necessary additions to wanting parts of machinery. He manufactures and puts up architectural iron work, fire proof doors, iron fences, aerial gratings and takes and fills contracts for steam and hot water heating. He is also agent for the Worthington pumps and United States injector. Mr. Patten was elected in 1888, and served five years as a member of the Salem water board. He was two years president of that body and during his service important additions and improvements were made to the system, six miles of new pipe being laid. His interest in public affairs has never been coupled with that of aiming at his own individual interests, and his activity as a member of the Board of Trade dates back to the organization in 1889, since which time he has served either as one of the directors or vice-presidents.

Salem Young Men's Christian Association.

Of the successful and world-wide work for the spiritual, mental and physical uplifting of young manhood done under the auspices of Young Men's Christian Associations, it is wholly unnecessary to treat at length in a community which has so vigorous an organization of this character in its midst. The local branch was formed Nov. 17, 1858, and until 1884 occupied rented rooms. In the latter year the association was incorporated and the present location was purchased, affording an excellent reading room, parlor, gymnasium, hall, etc., for the various departments. The building is open on week days from 9 A. M. until late in the evening, and men are always welcome. Besides 300 senior members, there are over 100 in the boys' branch, which was organized under the direction of its present leader, William H. Whipple, in 1869. The auxiliary includes 300 ladies, making a total of over 700 members and supporters. The present quarters have long been inadequate for the broadening work and for several years a fund has been growing for a new building which should meet the needs for a long time to come. In the spring of 1896, the Sanders and Hook estates at the corner of Essex and Sewall streets were purchased, and on Monday morning, August 2, 1897, William H. Whipple had the honor of turning the first shovelful of ground for the handsome structure now being erected on this site. The lot has a frontage of 150 feet, which will give four splendid stores in what is rapidly becoming the business centre of the city. On the Sewall street side will be a complete physical department, containing a large gymnasium, with visitors' gallery, running track, locker and bath rooms, and a beautiful swimming pool, lined with white tile. Here will also be the bowling alleys, bicycle room and a cage for ball practice. On the upper floor, approached by a marble staircase, a handsome auditorium seating about 800 will meet the needs of the entertainment and social sides of the work. There will also be a hall for the congress, boys' branch and small gatherings. Near by will be a kitchen and the Sewall street entrance to separate quarters for the boys, offices and committee rooms. The main reception room, parlor, reading and game rooms are to be over the stores on the Essex street front. On the third floor will be a camera room, rooms for classes in various educational lines, and dormitories. The construction will be such that a roof garden may be arranged, if desired. The open court in the rear will be devoted to

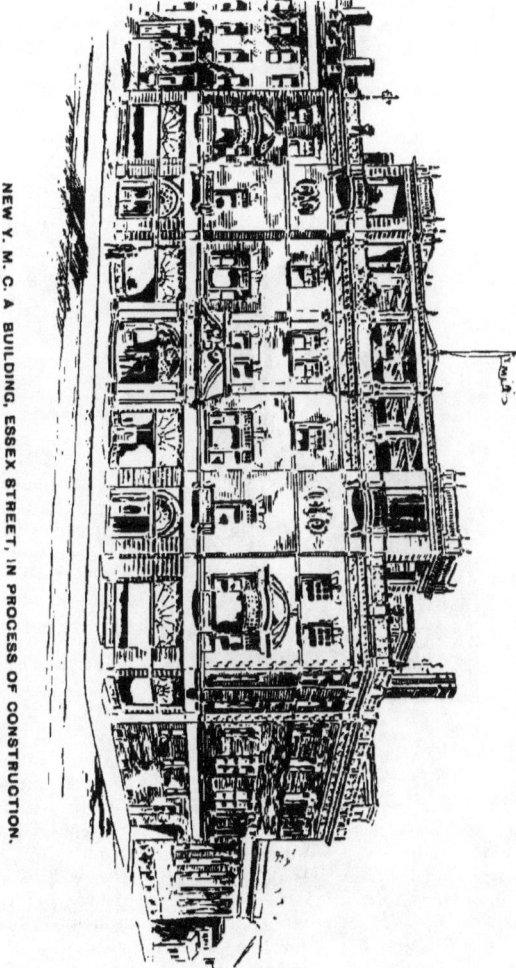

NEW Y. M. C. A BUILDING, ESSEX STREET, IN PROCESS OF CONSTRUCTION.

tennis and outdoor athletics generally, and will be accessible from Essex, Sewall and North streets. The front of the building will be of limestone for the first floor, with light brick above, and when completed will be in every way an ornament and credit to the city and one of the best of its kind in the country. A good beginning has been made, and as the enterprise is in the hands of substantial business men, it will commend itself to all as worthy of the most liberal financial aid at this time. In the neighborhood of $150,000 will be required to carry the work to completion. That other cities are appreciating this important work for young men and boys is shown by the fact that the association buildings of this country are valued at over $18,000,000. The officers of the Salem association are President, Matthew Robson; vice president, Leland H. Cole; recording secretary, Charles G. F. Coker; treasurer, Samuel J. Foster; auditor, Ezra F. Woodbury; general secretary, Charles H. Harrington; assistant secretary and physical instructor, Victor H. Mester.

CHARLES H. HARRINGTON.

Chas. H. Harrington, general secretary of the Salem Y. M. C. A., is now serving his third year here, but has been in association work since 1886. He is a native of New York state, was born in 1862, and devoted some five years to business life. He was engaged in the work in the state of New York for four years and at Camden, N. J., for over three years, at the latter place a magnificent institution having been built up. Mr. Harrington does not believe in temporary booms or in attempting enterprises beyond the facilities provided. Thus every association he has served is today on a successful basis, and he has every reason to expect equally good results from the liberal provision now being made for the future of his present field. It is the ambition of his life to see the local association housed in its new structure. Sept. 10, 1890, Mr. Harrington was united in marriage to Miss May White of New York city, and has three children. His home at 303 1-2 Essex street has become a favorite meeting place for the young, in whose welfare he is so much interested.

Essex Institute.

The Essex Institute began its work under that name fifty years ago. It was incorporated in 1848, but two county societies were merged in it, one of them, the Essex Historical, being formed seventy-five years ago. The accumulations of all those years have descended to the institute. Its officers are Robert S. Rantoul, president; Henry M. Brooks, secretary; W. O. Chapman, treasurer. The institute occupies the Daland house, Essex street, and the lower floor of Plummer hall. Its large collections in natural science, begun by the Natural History society in 1834, were, in 1867, deposited in trust with the Peabody Academy of Science. With that institution, as well as with the city library and the Athenæum, the institute co-operates on the most cordial terms. The functions of the institute are threefold. It supports a rare historical museum. It provides lectures and discussions for the winter months. It issues publications. Formerly, and for a long series of years, it conducted field meetings. To see Salem has now become part of a liberal education, and the visitors' book, which is interesting reading, shows that few strangers reach Salem who have not heard of the institute. Of course, a collection of pictures, relics, books and manuscripts, which has been growing three-quarters of a century in a community so intelligent and public-spirited as this, can hardly fail to offer, to everybody, something of interest. But perhaps the object possessing the greatest attractions is the little meeting house in the grounds behind, the frame of which was hewn out of the forest primeval in 1634, by the very first comers, after they had, under a broad and simple covenant, leagued themselves together, in 1629, to form the first Puritan church gathered on this continent. The institute gives away a succinct itinerary of Salem, sells a visitor's map for a few coppers, and of late years has published an illustrated guide book of two hundred pages which has reached its fortieth thousand. The institute conducts, during the winter, two lecture courses: one is for the public and is addressed by professional speakers of eminence who are disposed to contribute in this way to the success of so unique and popular an organization. On alternate Monday evenings, the institute entertains its own members with papers and discussions on local topics. The exchange list of the institute publications, American and foreign, numbers 260. One of the serials, the Historical Collections, has reached XXXIII volumes of about three hundred pages each. The other, the Bulletin, contains the proceedings of the meetings and such scientific papers as are forthcoming from members, from the Peabody Academy of Science, and other friendly sources. It is in its twenty-seventh volume. Such an institution as this cannot maintain its standard without friends, work, and funds. Its present rooms are full and it has the promise of splendid accessions as soon as proper space can be secured. It must grow or die. Thus far it has depended on the liberality and unrewarded labor of those persons, resident and non-resident, who see in it a bold experiment they would not willingly permit to fail. The hope of this country is, first, in the indomitable spirit of the people. After this, it is not in foreign conquest, nor in domestic institutions, nor in mediæval traditions, nor in political nor ecclesiastical dogma, nor in anything else save in the average intelligence and sound sense of the whole people. The institute is contributing to all. It is the growth of a self-sustained and courageous movement which could only grow up in a community with a history behind it and a bright out-

ESSEX INSTITUTE.

look ahead. The institute has a future before it as surely as the county has a future. The labors of such men and women as those who built it up, the hopes of such as have felt honored to fill its highest office, will not go for nothing. We may confidently predict that, with the return of better times, its needs will appeal to the benefactions of the affluent and that its perpetuity will be established.

Salem Gas Light Company.

The Salem Gas Light Company was chartered March 11, 1847, and organized April 4, 1850. The works were originally located on Northey street, the manufacturing being done there until April 16, 1890. An enlargement and extension becoming necessary and removal was made to the present location on the eastern side of Bridge street, near Beverly bridge, the new works being started April 8, 1890. The gas property includes the greater portion of the Pierce & Waite wharf and flats. For many years the concern from which the property derives its name conducted business at this point, sending vessels to all the world and becoming foremost among the great commercial houses of old Salem. The works overlook Beverly harbor, the coal supply of 1500 tons which the company annually consumes being delivered directly from vessels into the commodious sheds. The sheds are usually stocked in the summer months, although the wharf is available at practically all seasons. They are connected with the works by a long covered runway. The other principal buildings, with their dimensions are as follows: retort house, 50 x 65; engine and condenser house, 60 x 56; purity house, 61 x 56; meter house, 110 x 36 buckle house, 24 x 50. Besides these at the other houses, lime shed, pipe sheds, etc. At the works is a gasometer with a capacity of 65,000 cubic feet, and another 125,000 cubic feet, situated on North street. The company is to quadruple the works as contemplated shortly, or more than four times the present output. The machinery throughout is of the most modern and approved pattern. Over 2700 persons and firms in the city of Salem and the town of Peabody are now on the books as customers, the annual consumption being in the vicinity of 45,000,000 feet. The company has not yet seen fit to change from the manufacture of coal gas, and a large quantity of coke is supplied for domestic and business purposes. At the offices, 159 to 161½ Essex

HON. ROBERT S. RANTOUL, PRES. ESSEX INSTITUTE.

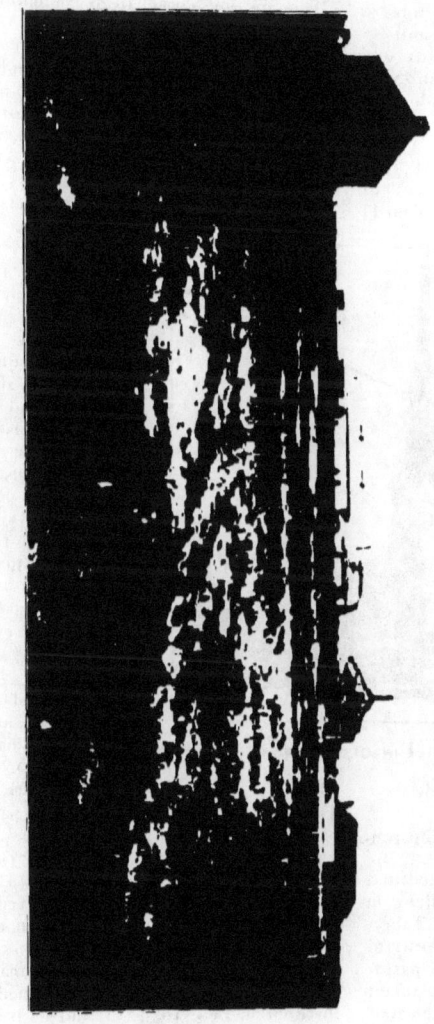

WORKS SALEM GAS LIGHT COMPANY.

street, a selected stock of gas stoves and improved lighting apparatus is carried in stock. Fifteen men are usually employed at the works and nearly thirty four miles of pipe are laid, the main pipe being of sixteen inch diameter. Since October 1, 1897, the price of gas per thousand feet has been $1.30, the same quantity once bringing $4.45. Since its organization, the company has had eight presidents, as follows: George Wheatland, George Choate, Stephen G. Wheatland, Francis Brown, Henry Gardner, William H. Jelly, John W. Leighton, and the present incumbent, Henry A. Hale. William H. Foster was the first clerk and treasurer, B. W. Shuman now holding that position. The dividends average five per cent. with the capital stock at $300,000. The directorate for 1897 is: H. A. Hale, J. P. Langmaid, C. F. Prichard, J. H. Smith, S. W. Winslow. George W. Mansfield has held the position of superintendent for the past six years. From its inception the gas company has been foremost in enterprise and has abundantly earned its reputation as one of the most successful and reliable corporations in this section.

Tabernacle Congregational Church.

The Tabernacle church originated in a division of the First church, Salem, in 1735. The first members of the Tabernacle church constituted the majority of the old church and included the pastor and other officers, and therefore claimed to be the First church, though ejected from their rights, as such, by the Magistrates of the colony. To put an end to a long and bitter controversy, in 1762, the majority surrendered the title, and the following year, voted to be called "the third church of Christ in Salem from this time forward." The first meeting house was destroyed by fire in 1774. The new one, corner of Washington and Federal street, modelled after Whitefield's Tabernacle in London, seems to have suggested the name by which the church came to be generally known, though it first appears on the records in 1786, and was gradually adopted, without any vote of the church. The second building was taken down in 1854, and the present wooden structure was erected the same year. The commodious chapel was built in 1868, and through the bequest of Miss Mary C. Anderson, the valuable parsonage, corner of Washington square and Oliver street, was secured. Since the division the list of pastors is: Revs. Samuel Fisk, Dudley Leavitt, John Huntington, Nathaniel Whitaker, D. D., Joshua Spaulding, Samuel Worcester, D. D., Elias Cornelius, D. D., John P. Cleaveland, D. D., Samuel M. Worcester, D. D., Charles R. Palmer, D. D., Hiram B. Putnam, DeWitt S. Clark, D. D. The average duration of these pastorates has been twelve years. The present membership of the church is 371 and of the Sunday school about 560. Honored and influential men have served as deacons and the church has been ever prominent in philanthropic and missionary work. The first foreign missionaries sent from this country were ordained in this church, Feb. 16, 1812, and its pastor at the time, Rev. Samuel Worcester, was the first secretary of the A. B. C. F. M., while Rev. Elias Cornelius was the first

TABERNACLE CHURCH.

secretary of the American Education society. The present officers are, besides the pastor: Deacons, Joseph H. Phippen, David Choate, Walter K. Bigelow, Ezra L. Woodbury, Charles E. Adams, Minot A. Holbrook; S. S. Superintendent, Frederick A. Fuller; Supt. of Primary Department, Susie E. Choate; Treasurer, Calvin R. Washburn; Clerk of the Proprietors, Arthur H. Phippen; Treasurer of the Proprietors, Geo. A. Shepard; Standing Committee, James F. Hale, Walter C. Packard, Calvin R. Washburn, Arthur H. Phippen, George A. Shepard; Choir, Geo. A. Shepard, organist, Henry L. Lefavour, James P. Hale, Mrs. Edwin R. Bigelow, Miss Bessie Curwen.

REV. DeWITT S. CLARK, D. D.

Of the large number of clergymen resident in Salem or vicinity, none is better known than Rev. Dr. DeWitt S. Clark, for nearly two decades pastor of the Tabernacle Congregational church. Dr. Clark has been conspicuously honored in his denominational relations and in the bestowal of such positions of public trust as membership upon the Salem school committee, with which board he has been connected since 1884, serving also as chairman of the sub-committee on the High school. Mr. Clark is the son of Rev. E. B. Clark, who for thirty-six years was pastor of the First Congregational church of Chicopee, in which place he was born September 11, 1841. He graduated from the Chicopee High school and Williston seminary, preparatory to entering Amherst college. Graduating with honor as a member of the Amherst class of '63, he devoted two years to teaching, in Upton and Saxonville, in charge of the High school in each place. With the determination of entering the ministry, Mr. Clark took a three years' course at Andover Theological seminary and was ordained and installed over the First Evangelical church of Clinton, November 11, 1868. Clinton was Mr. Clark's home until his acceptance of the call to Salem in 1878. Of the prosperity and harmony coincident with his Tabernacle pastorate, it is unnecessary to speak, as the facts are patent to all. He received the degree of D. D. from his Alma Mater in 1893. Dr. Clark is a corporate member of the A. B. C. F. M., a director of the Congregational Education society, trustee of the Massachusetts Bible society and director of the Congregational Board of Pastoral

Supply. He served as moderator at the session of the Mass. General Association of Congregational Churches at Springfield in 1890 and as preacher of the annual sermon at the meeting in Fall River. He was for one term president and for eight years secretary of the Essex Congregational club, is a member of the Boston Monday club, an organization publishing sermons annually upon the International Sunday school lessons, and is president of the Winthrop club of Boston. Dr. Clark has a vigorous literary talent and has contributed largely to the press.

South Congregational Church.

The South church has always held to 1735, when the Third church of Salem separated from the First, as the date of its beginning. While it was the smaller body of the two into which the Third church divided in 1774, in view of the fact that it continued in the Congregational order, while the other body became Presbyterian, it considered itself, and was adjudged by a council, entitled to keep the name "Third Church of Christ in Salem." But its attachment to that name became so slight that it was displaced in common usage by the name of South church. Its parish was incorporated in 1805 under the title, "Proprietors of the New South Meeting House in Salem," which was afterwards amended to "Proprietors of the South Church." The South church building was erected in 1804 and dedicated Jan. 1, 1805. As a specimen of colonial church architecture, it has been much admired, especially its shapely spire, designed by Samuel Mackintire, after models of Sir Christopher Wren. Its bell was made in London in 1807, and its crystal chandelier, now fitted with electric candles, also came from England. Since 1778 the South church has had only five pastors. For 110 years its pulpit was never vacant, each succeeding pastor beginning his service as colleague of his predecessor. Rev. Dr. Daniel Hopkins was settled as pastor in 1778 and held the office until his death in 1814, a term of thirty six years. Nine years previously, his son in law, Dr. Brown Emerson, was installed as associate pastor, assuming the full pastorate at Dr. Hopkins' demise, and was officially connected with the church until his death in 1872, a period of sixty seven years. In 1849, Rev. Dr. Israel E. Dwinell was settled as associate pastor with Dr. Emerson, and held office until his dismissal, because of failing health, in 1863, a term of fourteen years. Rev. Dr. Edward S. Atwood was settled as associate pastor with Dr. Emerson in 1864, and from Dr. Emerson's death, in 1875, was sole pastor until 1888, when he died. In February, 1889, about nine months after Dr. Atwood's death, Rev. James F. Brodie was installed in the pastorate, in which he still continues. In 1806, the scriptures were read for the first time as a part of the church services. In 1813, a Sabbath school class, one of the earliest in New England, was conducted by a member of the South church. The Sabbath school was formally organized in 1830. The church has a number of societies.

SOUTH CONGREGATIONAL CHURCH

REV. JAMES F. BRODIE.

Rev. James Fairbairn Brodie is now in his ninth year of service in this city, with a notably successful record in the pastorate and known most favorably by all because of his hearty sympathy and aid in all efforts tending to the uplifting of the needy. Rev. Mr. Brodie is of Scotch parentage on both the paternal and maternal sides and was born at Hammond, St. Lawrence county, New York, Sept. 24, 1854. He prepared for college at Gouveneur, Wesleyan, seminary, and graduated from Hamilton college, Clinton, N. Y., with first honors in the class of '76. He taught for two years at Greylock institute, Williamstown. With the intention of entering the ministry, Mr. Brodie took a divinity course at Union Theological seminary, New York city, from which he graduated in 1881. He was ordained at the Congregational church at Woodstock, Vt., Feb. 21, 1882. He was called to Salem in December, 1888, and installed Feb. 21 of the following year. Mr. Brodie takes high rank as a preacher, being gifted with an eloquent delivery. He is president of the Salem Relief committee and secretary of the Essex Congregational club.

Lafayette Street Methodist Episcopal Church.

Jesse Lee visited Salem July 12, 1790, and preached the first Methodist sermon heard in the city. There was a small company of Methodists present, connected with the churches in Marblehead and Lynn. The first Methodist class in Salem was formed by Samuel Berry, a layman, in 1815. During the years 1818 and 1819 Jesse Fillmore, then stationed in Marblehead, preached several times in the city. He was appointed to Salem, June 29, 1822, and found there a class of twenty-five members. A lot of land was bought on Sewall street, on which a small church was erected. This was used most of the time as a place of worship until 1841. In that year thirty Methodists were organized into a class by Rev. N. S. Spaulding, and under his leadership proceeded to erect a new church on Union street. It was dedicated Jan. 8, 1841, and cost $2,060. Rev. Daniel Wise preached the dedication sermon. Rev. Luman Boyden was appointed to the charge in 1851. He found that a new church was needed and decided that it

REV. JAMES F. BRODIE.

LAFAYETTE ST M. E. CHURCH.

should be built at the corner of Lafayette and Harbor streets. A lot was purchased in that place and the corner stone of the new church laid May 12, 1852. The building was completed and dedicated in January, 1853. James F. Almy, in his history of Salem Methodism, says, "The house was thronged with the very best people of the city, and Bishop Baker preached the sermon." The house was thoroughly remodeled and repaired in 1893-4, during the pastorate of Rev. George F. Eaton, D. D., and is now one of the most attractive and convenient in the conference. The cost of the renovation was about $13,000. Two sessions of the New England conference have been held in this church, one in 1856, during the pastorate of Rev. Daniel Richards, and another in 1895, during the pastorate of Rev. George S. Chadbourne, D. D. The list of pastors, with date of appointments, follows: Jesse Fillmore, 1822; Epaphras Kibby, 1825; Henry Mayo, 1826; Nathan B. Spaulding, 1827; Joseph B. Brown, 1829; A. Want, 1830; N. S. Spaulding, 1832; Jefferson Hamilton, 1833; C. S. McReading, 1834; G. Pickering, 1835; J. W. Downing, 1836; Stephen G. Hyler, 1838; A. D. Sargent, 1839; N. S. Spaulding, 1840; Joseph A. Merrill, 1842; D. K. Merrill, 1843; Horace Moulton, 1845; F. Crandle, 1846; David Winslow, 1847; J. W. Perkins, 1849; Lyman Bowden, 1851; A. D. Merrill, 1853; Daniel Richards, 1854; L. A. Adams, 1856; A. F. Herrick, 1858; John H. Mansfield, 1859; E. A. Manning, 1861; Gershom F. Cox, 1862; Lorenzo Crowell, 1864; S. F. Chase, 1867; Daniel Dorchester, 1869; J. S.

REV. DILLON BRONSON.

Whedon, 1872; George L. Collyer, 1875; Daniel Steele, 1878; George W. Mansfield, 1880; W. P. Ray, 1883; S. L. Gracey, 1886; George A. Phinney, 1889; George F. Eaton, 1892; George S. Chadbourne, 1894; Dillon Bronson, 1897. The present official members are: Trustees, Charles S. Clark, C. H. Glazier, George W. Lane, James F. Almy, D. W. Hamilton, Mager Page, J. A. Hurd, N. Abbott, W. Bickerton; stewards, D. W. Hamilton, Fred M. Page, L. A. King, W. B. Bigelow, W. L. Packard, G. W. Pollock, George W. Lane, J. A. Hurd, W. M. Smith, C. H. Glazier, Frank A. Page, Mrs. Emma S. Almy, Mrs. Helen J. Butler; class leaders, C. H. Glazier, W. W. Hamilton; superintendent of Sunday school, James F. Almy. The Epworth League officers are: President, Arthur Sawyer; first vice president, Mrs. A. D. Pitman; second vice president, Fred Daley; third vice president, Herbert Davison; fourth vice president, Miss Bessie Kimball; secretary, Miss Florence Glazier; treasurer, Mrs. Frank A. Page.

REV. DILLON BRONSON

was born in 1863 at Wyoming, Iowa, a town founded and named by his father, Hon. James A. Bronson. At fourteen years of age he graduated from the Wyoming High school, and at twenty from Cornell college, Iowa, the youngest in a class of twenty-four. Mr. Bronson came to Boston in 1885 and graduated from the Boston University School of Theology in 1888. Though youngest in the class again, he was chosen by the faculty for one of the two commencement speakers. A few days after graduation, he was called by the official board of the Bromfield Street church, Boston, to supply the pulpit until the following spring, when he joined the conference and was excused to attend school in Germany. In connection with a year's study at the University of Berlin, where he often preached in the German language, he made a two years' tour of the globe, visiting the principal mission stations of the orient, collecting curios, photographs and stereopticon views which have greatly aided him in the preparation of popular lectures on travel. On his return to America in 1892 he was appointed pastor at Newton, where he completed his fifth year, being one of the seven pastors among the 250 in the conference who were changed in 1897 by reason of the expiration of the time limit. During Mr. Bronson's pastorate at Newton, the society doubled in membership, greatly increased its benevolent collections and pledged over $42,000 for the elegant new church recently completed. In 1894, Mr. Bronson married Susan Hall Peirce, daughter of Silas Peirce, the Boston banker and wholesale grocer. Mrs. Bronson makes an ideal pastor's wife.

Second Church in Salem (Unitarian.)

The church now worshiping in the edifice properly known as the East church was formed by the union of the old East church and the Independent Congregational church in Barton square. Upon the resignation of Rev. Edward D. Towle of the East church in June, 1897, to take charge of the new Second Unitarian church in Brookline, a movement was started to secure a union of the above mentioned churches, retaining Rev. Alfred Manchester, of the church on Barton square, as pastor of the new organization, to be known as the Second Church in Salem, thus preserving the traditions of one of the historic religious societies of the city and increasing the efficiency of the cause which the two churches represented. The East church was an offshoot from the First church. Its first house of worship, at the corner of Essex and Hardy streets, was opened for public services in May, 1718, and was used for that purpose until the dedication of the present structure, Jan. 2, 1846. Under Dr. William Bentley in 1785, the church became practically Unitarian. The Independent Congregational church in Barton square was dedicated in December, 1824, and has been Unitarian from the beginning. After an honorable career of nearly three-quarters of a century, it unites with the ancient East church to form the Second Church in Salem, with every prospect of a strong and influential organiza-

SECOND CHURCH UNITARIAN

tion which shall preserve and increase every good characteristic for which the two uniting societies have stood in this community for so many years. The organization, as completed in November, 1897, is: Clerk, Frank S. Perkins, treasurer, Joseph H. M. Edwards; executive committee, Henry M. Batchelder, David N. Pousland, John P. Reynolds, Henry P. Moulton, Wm. H. Gove.

REV. ALFRED MANCHESTER.

Rev. Alfred Manchester was born in Portsmouth, R. I., Nov. 16, 1846. His father was George Manchester and his grandfather, Hon. John Manchester, both of whom throughout their lives were identified with town and state affairs, being active in anti-slavery and other progressive movements. On his mother's side, Mr. Manchester is a direct descendant of the John Coggeshall, who, a year before Roger Williams founded Providence, founded Portsmouth in the same state. His mother was Phoebe T. Coggeshall, daughter of John H. Coggeshall, Esq. Mr. Manchester attended the schools of his native town and the High school of Pawtucket. He entered the Boston School for the Ministry and after partially completing its course of study, took the full course of the divinity school of Harvard University, from which he graduated in 1872. From 1873 to 1878 he was pastor of the Unitarian church in Fairhaven. From Jan. 1, 1878 to May 1, 1893, he was pastor of the Olney Street church (Unitarian) of Providence. During this pastorate he was identified with many benevolent and philanthropic institutions, being active on their boards of management. In May, 1893, he became pastor of the Barton Square church in this city, and upon the union with the East church, he became pastor of the new church. He has visited the old world, having made a tour of eastern Palestine, going as far east as Damascus. He has given many lectures on his journeyings. Mr. Manchester is an active Mason and is chaplain of Essex Lodge, F. & A. M., of this city. He is also an Odd Fellow, retaining his membership in lodge and encampment in the jurisdiction of Rhode Island, where he was grand chaplain for several years. During his Salem pastorate he has acted as secretary of the Essex Unitarian conference and is now secretary of the Essex Unitarian club.

REV. ALFRED MANCHESTER.

SALEM 1626-1897

ADVENT CHRISTIAN CHURCH.

Advent Christian Church.

For many years prior to the formation of the present church in 1875, meetings of people of the Advent faith had been held in Salem. For some years these meetings were held in Holyoke and Hardy halls, the old church on Herbert street being purchased in 1885 and occupied until 1890. At that time a change became desirable; the Herbert street building was sold and the present structure at the corner of North street and Mead court built, largely through the efforts of Rev. G. F. Haines, at that time pastor of the church. New interest and increasing prosperity have fully justified the change. The last year, under the pastorate of Rev. J. W. Davis, has been an exceptionally prosperous one, thirty-eight new members having been added, making the total membership 167. The pastors previous to those already named were Revs. Charles Goodrich, George W. Sederquist and Elmer N. Hinckley. Two years since, the church was incorporated, which greatly simplifies the work. The Sunday school numbers 130 members, Frank J. Rich and Jennie Davis serving as superintendent and secretary respectively. The Loyal Workers, an organization of young people, has fifty-five active members. The present church officers are: Pastor, Rev. James W. Davis; elders, Rev. E. N. Hinckley, Norman H. Sederquist; clerk, Alpheus C. Locke; treasurer, Rev. E. N. Hinckley; committee, Charles C. Morse, F. J. Rich, William H. Stanwood, Albert F. Hall, Asaph H. Higgins; deacons, Charles Mooney, Daniel Mooney.

REV. JAMES W. DAVIS

is one of the leading clergymen of his denomination, as was shown by his selection as one of seven to represent the Advent body at the parliament of religions at Chicago in 1893. Mr. Davis' early relations were with the Methodists, uniting with that church when but ten years old. Thrown upon his own resources at an early age, he secured an academic education, was licensed to preach in 1872 and served as pastor of Methodist churches at Naugatuck and at Roxbury. In 1885 his views changed, causing him to affiliate with the Connecticut Advent Christian conference. Mr. Davis' first pastorate with the Adventists was at Bridgeport, accepting the call there in 1887 and remaining until his removal to Salem, late in 1896. He is a war veteran, a past commander of the Wadham Post, G. A. R., of Waterbury, was chaplain of the department of Connecticut for four

REV. JAS. W. DAVIS.

years and later had the rank of inspector-general on the staff of Commander-in-Chief Burdett. He has also had an extended business experience. Sept. 17, 1865, Mr. Davis married Miss Addie Hoyt of Pound Ridge, N. Y., and has three children. As a pastor he is a thoroughly consecrated and successful worker, devoted to his church and parish, deeply versed in the scriptures, and commands the respect and esteem of all, both in and out of his congregation.

The North Society (Unitarian).

The North society was formed on account of a division among the members of the First parish regarding pastoral relations. In May, 1772, fifty two persons were dismissed from the First church and formed the new society. The first building was situated on the south-east corner of Lynde and North streets and was opened for public worship August 23, 1772; in this church the society remained for sixty-five years until the erection of the present building on Essex street. Dr. Thomas Barnard, the first pastor, was installed January 13th, 1773, and until his death in 1814 he remained in charge of the parish. These were stirring times and when on a Sunday in February, 1775, a battalion of British troops marched past his church towards the North bridge, Dr. Barnard, at the head of his congregation, hastened to the spot, where matters were fast assuming a serious aspect; he argued with Colonel Leslie and finally suggested the compromise which prevented bloodshed. John Emery Abbot for four years, John Brazer for twenty-five years, Octavius B. Frothingham for eight years, and Charles Low for two years, followed Dr. Barnard; then came the pastorate of Edmund B. Willson, who was installed June 5, 1859. Mr. Willson was greatly beloved by his parish and the community. At the close of his thirty sixth anniversary sermon he was stricken in his pulpit and died a few days later, on June 13, 1895. The present pastor is George D. Latimer, installed as assistant minister May 3, 1895, succeeding to the pastorate shortly after Mr. Willson's death. The rolls of the society have always borne the names of persons among the most prominent in the city; in old times famous merchants, in later days many men of affairs.

NORTH CHURCH.

St. Peter's Episcopal Church.

The first edifice of St. Peter's parish was erected at the corner of St. Peter and Brown streets in 1733 and the present structure one hundred years later. The church is of stone and the architecture of the English gothic style. It is now the generally accepted opinion that the first religious services conducted in Salem were those in charge of Rev. John Lyford, a minister of the church of England, who came with Gov. Roger Conant in 1625, having been previously located at Plymouth. From this date up to the time of the formation of St. Peter's parish, Episcopal services were probably held with greater or less regularity. During the war of the revolution it became necessary to suspend services, so intense was the feeling against the mother country, and the property of the parish suffered somewhat from violence. The old bell was first rung in 1740 and still hangs in the tower, a chime of ten bells being placed in position in 1885. In the old edifice[1] was the first organ ever heard in a Salem church. The tablets containing the Apostles' Creed, Lord's Prayer and Ten Commandments, which were painted in 1738 for the old church, are still preserved, as well as the large folio volume of Common Prayer given the church in 1744 by the Rt. Hon. Sir Arthur Onslow, then speaker of the house of commons. In the church yard, near the street, are many stones of interest, dating back to the middle of the eighteenth century. For the first few years after the erection of the original building, the parish was ministered to by neighboring clergy, the first rector, Rev. Charles Brockwell, A. M., having been settled in 1738. The succeeding pastors, with date of settlement, follow: Rev. William McGilchrist, 1747; Rev. Nathaniel Fisher, 1782; Rev. Thomas Carlisle, 1817; Rev. Henry W. Ducachet, 1824; Rev. Thomas W. Coit, D. D., LL. D., 1826; Rt. Rev. Alexander V. Griswold, bishop of the eastern diocese, 1829; Rev. John A. Vaughn, D. D., 1834; Rev. Charles Mason, D. D., 1837; Rev. William R. Babcock, 1848; Rev. George Leeds, 1853; Rev. William R. Pickman, 1860; Rev. James O. Scripture, 1865; Rev. Edward M. Gushee, 1870; Rev. Charles Arey, D. D., 1875; Rev. Henry Bedinger, 1891. The present officers of the parish are: Francis Cox, senior warden; Charles F. Curwen, junior warden; David Allen, William F. Gavet, Fred G. Pousland, William P. McMullan, John P. Peabody, William O. Safford, L. V. Shaw, Louis F. Gavet, J. Orne Ryder, vestrymen; Lewis F. Allen, clerk and treasurer.

ST. PETER'S CHURCH.

REV. HENRY BEDINGER was born in the Shenandoah valley, about nine miles above Harper's Ferry, and was there during the stirring times of the civil war. In the fall of 1870 he entered the University of Virginia, later going to the General Theological seminary (Episcopal,) New York. He was ordained deacon in 1875 and priest two years later. His rectorates have been at Kittaning, Pa., Matteawan, N. Y., and St. Peter's in this city, assuming his last charge in January, 1891.

St. Joseph's Roman Catholic Church and Parish.

Rev. Gabriel Druillites, a Jesuit and native of France, visited Naumkeag as guest of Gov. John Endicott as early as 1651, but it was not until over a century later that the first considerable number of French Catholics were to be found here, some 150 arriving from Arcadia, of whom

ST. JOSEPH'S R. C. FRENCH CHURCH

the larger part returned to Canada within a short time. The few who remained doubtless were represented in the congregation which assembled at the first mass ever celebrated in Salem May 6, 1860,

Rev. John Thayer officiating. No attempt was made to furnish the French-speaking Catholics with instructive services until June 30, 1873. Upon that date Rev. Matthew H. Sougrew, Justice

ST. JOSEPH'S PAROCHIAL SCHOOL

of Providence, but then stationed in Salem, assembled the French Catholics in the basement of the Immaculate Conception church and held a service for their particular benefit. Fr. Harkins had a complete mastery of the French language. He remained in charge of the work until May, 1875, when Rev. John Talbot was appointed to succeed him. Fr. Talbot's suggestion for the purchase of land in South Salem with a view to the erection of a church met with such opposition that he left the city and Fr. Harkins again took charge. The pastorate was later held by Revs. O. Boucher and Francis X. L. Vezina. During the administration of the latter, the Lafayette street property was purchased, services having been held for some years previously at the Seamen's Bethel on Herbert street, which had been altered for church purposes. The present fine structure was opened with notable exercises, Aug. 25, 1885. Shortly after, Rev. Joseph O. Gadoury was appointed assistant to Fr. Vezina, and upon the retirement of the latter on account of ill health, assumed full charge of the parish, remaining to the present time. In the development of St. Joseph's parish since the coming of Fr. Gadoury to the city, is the life work of one man. The property now used as the parochial residence has been bought and fitted up and the school building, erected in 1892 on Harbor square, accommodates some 900 pupils, twenty Grey Nuns of Montreal acting as teachers. A convent is adjacent. The leading auxiliary societies are the St. Jean Baptiste, Union of St. Joseph, and League of the Sacred Heart, all having a large and influential membership. The seeds scattered upon the ground so few years ago, comparatively, have had a mighty expansion. The French population is approximately one sixth that of the entire city, residing largely in the territory east of Lafayette and south of Harbor streets. Of the activity and success of this element in every department of public life, it is useless to dwell further than to remark that citizens of French birth and extraction are among the leaders in every substantial enterprise in Salem at the present time.

REV. JOSEPH O. GADOURY was born in the province of Quebec, July 17, 1851, his early education being received at the schools of the district. He graduated from Joliet college with the class of '70 and the same year entered St. Joseph's provincial seminary at Troy, N. Y., studying philosophy and theology. After a course at Assumption seminary in Canada, he was ordained by Archbishop Fabre, July 16, 1876, and spent three years at the Assumption institution as professor of literature. Fr. Gadoury was appointed assistant rector at Beauharnois, near Montreal, and later served in a similar capacity at St. Vincent de Paul's church, Montreal, remaining there until his coming to Salem. Fr. Gadoury, as the spiritual adviser and leader of the immense parish of some 6,000 souls, has gained the love and esteem of his people, and by his

REV. JOS. O. GADOURY.

frank and unassuming manner, tireless energy and executive capacity, commands the respect of the entire community, regardless of denomination.

REV. LOUIS J M. LEVESQUE

REV. LOUIS M. LEVESQUE was born in the province of Quebec 1855 and graduated at Joliet college 1878. He studied theology at the University of Ottawa and was ordained by Archbishop Tachè, July 20, 1881. He acted as chaplain at St. Vincent de Paul penitentiary for one year and as assistant pastor at Joliet for two years. He next was stationed at Peterborough, in the province of Ontario, as pastor of the French congregation, residing at the bishop's palace. Six years were spent in the diocese of Sherbrooke in pastoral work, and two years in the state of New York as chaplain of Sisters of Mercy. Fr. Levesque has been assistant at St. Joseph's since September, 1893.

REV. JOSEPH A. PELTIER.

Fr. Gadoury's second assistant is Rev. Joseph A. Peltier, who came to Salem in June, 1895. He was born in the province of Quebec in 1866, thirteen years of his life having been spent at Joliet college, at which institution he studied theology. Like Frs. Gadoury and Levesque, Fr. Peltier was ordained by the great Archbishop Tachè, that ceremony occurring May 27, 1893. The period intervening before his assignment to this city was spent at Joliet college as instructor in Latin and Greek, also acting for part of the time as music teacher. For

REV. JOS. A. PELTIER.

Rev. James L. Hill, D. D.

Dr. Hill's first success was in housing good parents from whom to be born. His father, a graduate of Bowdoin and Andover, went out as a home missionary to the territory of Iowa as a member of the far-famed Iowa band and gave the first dollar to found Iowa college, which has been now for many years the mother of patriots and missionaries. His mother entered upon the labors and privations of this pioneer life with whole-hearted enthusiasm and devotion, exclaiming "Somebody must be built into these

REV. JAMES L. HILL, D. D.

employs more teachers than any other state in our proud domain, with the single exception of New York. Remembering his father's gift to Iowa college, when the Dacotah Band were leaving New England, Dr. Hill gave one of them the first dollar a library fund to the college. In 1896 Dr. Hill gave the commencement address at Washburn college, Topeka, Kansas, of which Mr. Scoville, the president of the board of trustees, said as he conferred the degrees upon the graduates, "This was an address well worth crossing a state to hear and well worth crossing these broad United States to deliver." By a curious chain of circumstances this commencement address has led to a great multiplicity of lecture engagements as far west as Kansas, where the coming month of January is to be spent, and in New England, which involves an absence from home for two weeks at a time, when every evening will be taken by an appointment. Dr. Hill has given over three hundred convention and anniversary addresses before societies of endeavor. He was one of four clergymen who went to England in 1891 to make addresses and to plant societies of christian endeavor. He founded the society in Old Boston in England. While absent on this errand his Alma Mater conferred on him the title of doctor of divinity. He has been a trustee of the United Society of Christian Endeavor from the beginning, and of him the editor of the Golden Rule said, "No one is more popular on a christian endeavor platform than Rev. James L. Hill, D. D., and few are in greater demand." In its published vote of thanks Post 66, G. A. R., makes this public record: "It has not been the province of this post ever to have since its organization such an oration delivered to them and, sir, it stirred the same feeling of patriotism in our hearts that caused us to leave our homes in '61-'65." Dr. Hill preached the election sermon upon "The Growth of Government" before the governor and senate and house of representatives of Massachusetts, and the governor said that it was the best election sermon he had heard during his term of office. Before graduating from Andover Dr. Hill was called to Lynn, where he remained twelve years, and thence to the Mystic church in Medford, where he preached for eight years, beside doing a vast amount of outside work with voice and pen. His contributions to the religious press make four hundred and fifty pages, as large as those of an atlas, and this, to say nothing of scores of leaflets and addresses. He has the habit of industry and the modern methods of christian martyrs, and the new movements in the religious world have given him a wide and inviting and welcome opportunity. During the last summer he supplied the united congregations of five churches in Jersey City for six Sundays, and the summer before he occupied the pulpit of the Second Presbyterian church, where he performed similar service. At the time of the World's Fair the state of Iowa asked him officially to supply a complete set of his works to compose a part of the exhibit of his native state. In conjunction with his brother, who is superintendent of the Iowa Hospital for the Insane, he has given $2,000 to found the Hill prize, which is given at each commencement by his Alma Mater for the promotion of excellence in extemporaneous address. This contest is proving one of the most popular and inspiring events of commencement week. Dr. Hill, who resides at No. 225 Lafayette street, thinks he can say what no other resident in this city can affirm, that he came to Salem deliberately after years of consideration, solely because he believed it was the pleasantest place to make a home in this state or in any other. He makes the point that the residents in communities too closely suburban to Boston have a divided interest and that such residential districts are lacking in place-pride and local esprit de corps.

Rev. Edwin P. Farnham.

Rev. Edwin P. Farnham, pastor of the First Baptist church, was born at Morris, Litchfield county, Conn., in 1849. He taught school in that state and prepared for college at Suffield academy, graduated from Brown with the class of '73, and was class orator and member of the Phi Beta Kappa society. The following year he entered Rochester Theological seminary, graduating in 1877. In October of that year, Mr. Farnham began work in his first pastorate with the Friendship Street Baptist church of Providence. Receiving a unanimous call to the Warburton Avenue Baptist church, Yonkers, N. Y., he accepted the same in January, 1883, remaining for a little over three

(Churches Continued on Page 91.)

Boston and Maine Railroad.

The city of Salem was opened up to railroad communication August 27, 1838. The transportation facilities were then in the hands of the Eastern Railroad, and so continued to 1883, when the property passed into the control of the great Boston & Maine system. Salem is now on the Eastern division of the Boston & Maine, afforded with passenger and freight facilities befitting its immense and growing interests. The management of the road has ever been alive to the needs and demands of the city, and to this, in a great degree, can be credited the position in which the historic old community now finds herself among the sister municipalities of this and adjoining states. Besides the main line of the Eastern division, extending from Boston on the south to Portland on the north, a branch line reaches to the neighboring town of Peabody, where, in turn, are three lines—to South Reading, to Lawrence and to Lowell. Of these lines, Salem is practically the eastern terminus, and when one considers the immense amount of business which must be transacted between these points, some idea of the importance of the city as a railroad center may be obtained. Every reasonable demand is abundantly supplied by the alert and considerate Boston & Maine officials. From the passenger station in Salem thirty-eight trains arrive and depart daily, excellent service and connections being given between and at terminal points in all directions. The main passenger depot is one of the most unique and substantial structures on the road, or in fact in this part of the country. It is situated at the junction of Norman and Washington streets, convenient to the business center, car lines, etc. The depot was built in 1847 from designs imported from England. In 1882 fire badly damaged the building, but the work of re-construction was along the original lines, and the depot stands today as interesting as ever. On the front are two large towers, of simple but impressive design and strength. Trains enter the station under a stone arch connecting the two towers. In the head-house are offices of the local management. On both sides of the track are ample waiting rooms and conveniences. A long train shed extending to the south affords protection to passengers and baggage. The auxiliary stations within the city limits are Atlantic, North Street and Carltonville. Harry A. Whitehead is the efficient general agent at this point; Lewis W. Marden, ticket agent, and William E. Felton, baggage master. The freight business is under the general supervision of C. A. Chandler, who began his duties here under the old Eastern regime. The mention of the freight department brings to attention the great volume to which this traffic has grown. Salem is a port of entry, and during the year an immense amount of material for the textile centers of Lowell and Lawrence and other busy cities, is received here by water and re-shipped over the Boston & Maine. Thus, in addition to local business, the city is a distributing point to a large manufacturing district. The freight depot is located on Mill street. About twenty-five acres are included in the freight yard bounds and about three hundred cars are handled daily, giving employment to several switching engines and crews. The average monthly tonnage is: Forwarded, 25,000 tons; received, 21,000 tons. Every facility in the line of warehouses, freight sheds, water front, wharves, etc., is at the disposal of the railroad. On Bridge street is a large repair shop of the company, comprising five large and numerous smaller buildings. About 250 men are regularly employed here, the annual repair list comprising about 3500 freight and 300 passenger cars. A machine shop is also located here. Sylvanus R. Arey is general foreman in charge. G. L. R. French, roadmaster of the Eastern division, and H. F. Russell, superintendent of bridges and buildings, have offices and make their headquarters in Salem. In the vicinity of ten miles of track are laid in the city, and employment is given to between 600 and 700 men, a large por-

BOSTON & MAINE DEPOT, SALEM.

SALEM 1626-1897

BOSTON & MAINE FREIGHT YARDS, SALEM.

tion of whom reside in Salem or immediate vicinity. The advantages of a municipality having as an ally a great and progressive railway system is nowhere more obvious than in the city of Salem.

The Lynn & Boston Railroad Company.

The company which now controls the street transportation of passengers in Salem and vicinity is well worthy of extended notice in this volume. Its growth has been marvellous and in harmony with the progress of the age, providing unrivalled facilities for public pleasure and convenience. 1896 transported over 25,000,000 passengers over its vast system. The horse cars have given place entirely to the modern and expensively fitted trolley cars; and the application of electricity as a motive power has contributed much to the convenience of the travelling public. This power was first applied to the cars of the company in 1888, this being the first road in the state to discard the old methods of locomotion, and to "harness the lightning" to do its bidding. In 1892 the company obtained possession of the Naumkeag Street Railway Co. and the Essex Electric Street Railway Company, the two roads then operating in Salem and its immediate vi-

TERMINUS OF L. & B. R. R. SALEM WILLOWS.

The Lynn & Boston Railroad Company was incorporated by an act of the Massachusetts Legislature, which became a law April 6, 1859. At the time of its incorporation, the company owned forty horses and eight cars, which were used on a track running from Boston to Lynn, and comprising a total mileage, single track, of about thirteen miles. In comparison with this meagre showing, the recent statistics are highly creditable. The company now has a track mileage of 163 miles, owns 588 cars, and in the year cinity. Since the absorption of these, the Lynn & Boston management has been constantly making improvements and the change has been decidedly beneficial to Salem. The roadbed here, or the greater portion of it, has been practically rebuilt, and on sections where the travel is heaviest, rails have been laid weighing ninety pounds to the yard and costing, including labor and other auxiliary expense, $18,000 for each mile of single track laid. Another improvement has been made by the erection of a large and commodious power station, equipped with all the latest appliances, an interior view of which building is here shown. Continual extensions and absorptions of other roads have so enlarged the system that the company now operates on a vast network of tracks in eighteen cities and towns of Eastern Massachusetts, as follows: Boston, Chelsea, Everett, Malden, Melrose, Stoneham, Woburn, Revere, Saugus, Lynn, Swampscott, Salem, Marblehead, Peabody, Danvers, Beverly, Wenham and Hamilton. From many of these places connections can be made with other roads, and long journeys may be taken by trolley, at an average cost of about half what is charged on steam railroads, and with much greater pleasure to the average traveller, especially during the summer season. Trolley parties have long since become the fashion, the idea being to charter a special car and take a long journey by this mode of locomotion. A recent itinerary of such a party included a trip from New Bedford, Mass., to Gloucester, Mass., and another, fully as long, was from Taunton, Mass., to Nashua, N. H. The motion of the trolley car, being easy and comfortable, is just swift enough to be healthful and exhilarating. Besides regularly organized parties, there are family parties and individuals innumerable who ride on the trolley cars purely for pleasure, and to the student of nature or the sight-seeing tourist who may wish to view the beautiful cities and towns on

POWER STATION OF THE L. & B. R. R. AT SALEM.

the North Shore to best advantage, we recommend an inspection of these beauties, in proper season, from the open electric cars of this company. But the benefits derived from a great railway system like that operated by the Lynn & Boston company are practical as well as sentimental. Suburbs are opened up and made more accessible from the cities, thereby diffusing the population, improving the health of the people and largely increasing the number of house-owners. Since the introduction of electricity as a motive power, the distances to which the company can afford to carry passengers for the minimum or five cent fare have greatly increased. This is especially true in Salem, where there is a liberal free transfer system in vogue, rendering it possible to travel between Salem and all immediate suburbs at the lowest rate. Salem is a retail center for a population of 100,000 people, and the service of the Lynn & Boston Railroad company is appreciated by Salem's retail merchants and other tradesmen, as it has enabled this city not only to hold

that it is possible to make a journey to Franklin Park without passing through the city of Boston. This may be done by taking a car through Lynn to Melrose and Stoneham, thence to Winchester and Arlington, and from there to the park named, but one can also pass through the new subway to Scollay Square, Boston. One may also go to Lowell from Salem, or to Brockton. A very popular route is from Marblehead to Scollay Square, Boston, a trip that may be taken without changing of cars. In the near future it is expected that one will be able to go from Salem to Boston without

WAITING ROOM OF L. & B. H. R., SALEM

choose to patronize the trolley cars at certain seasons of the year. It may be readily imagined that the finances of a street railway company require the most careful supervision as to details, especially as the margin of profit on each passenger carried is exceedingly small, being less than half of one cent on each five-cent fare. The rolling-stock, roadbed, equipments and service of the Lynn & Boston corporation compare favorably with other roads and rank high among the street railways of the world. As an illustration of the progressive methods of the company, it may be mentioned that fifty-two electrical car equipments have been discarded, and the latest improved motors, made by the General Electric company, have been substituted. Many of their new motors are in use here in Salem. The corporation has the following executive officers: President, Amos F. Breed; vice president, E. Francis Oliver; treasurer, Charles Williams; general manager, E. C. Foster. Salem is represented on the board of directors by Hon. H. P. Moulton. Much of the great success of the road is doubtless due to

ROBIN DAMON, PROPRIETOR SALEM EVENING NEWS.

its able management, and especially to the careful executive supervision of General Manager Foster, who gives his personal attention to all the details of the vast business of the company, keeping in constant touch with all parts of the system.

The Salem Evening News.

Welcomed into nearly every home in Salem and the cities and towns contiguous, a brief history of the paper's seventeen years of life must possess an interest for the 90,000 daily readers. They have been years of struggle and triumph, in which, from a very humble beginning, there has been constant progress to the present position. Conceived in the belief that there was a demand for a trustworthy disseminator of general information regarding the world and its inhabitants, their manner of living and their daily actions, The News was launched by its present proprietor on October 16, 1880, the size being about one-twelfth of the present form. The modest venture was cordially received by the public, and ere long there was plenty of evidence that a popular chord had been touched, and the music of success could be heard - softly, at first, but, like the oncoming of a mighty army, gradually increasing in volume, until it burst forth in the grandeur of a magnificent symphony. Before triumph was achieved there were many days of struggle and hardship, which at times seemed too burdensome for human endurance. Persistency, however, accompanied with wisdom, brings success in all undertakings. Thus amid many vicissitudes, in which despondency never found a place, the desired end was ever kept in view, and the determination to give to Salem a daily paper worthy of the city and of its place in history never faltered. An appreciative public generously supported the effort, and from the humble, though ambitious beginning, The News rose in favor, until in a comparatively brief period it had found a place at every fireside, in every office and workshop, and in all places where men were wont to congregate. The News Publishing Company was formed in the autumn

OFFICE OF THE SALEM NEWS, WASHINGTON STREET.

of 1880, with Robin Damon as treasurer and general manager. A sample copy, giving a prospectus of the new venture, was issued from the job printing office of Mr. Damon, in the Browne Block, Essex street, and on October 16, 1880, the first regular number was sent forth from that office. The stockholders of the new enterprise soon wearied of their interests, and the property was purchased by Robin Damon and Charles H. Cochrane, so continuing until August 25, 1881, when Mr. Cochrane retired and Mr. Damon became sole proprietor. From that date the latter until the next year, when a larger press was installed, and so on, until at the present time there are facilities at command capable of turning out 25,000 papers an hour. Business increased rapidly, the merchants of the city learning the value of printer's ink, when employed in a popular medium. The four-column paper, 10 x 15 inches, was enlarged another column, and the size to 11½ x 16. Two months later another column was added and the size increased to 13 x 19 inches. On June 1, 1882, another column became a necessity, and

INTERIOR BUSINESS OFFICE, SALEM EVENING NEWS.

has been alone in the ownership of the property. A small Kidder job press was equal to the task of printing the first numbers, but soon the faithful little machine failed to meet the demand. Business had so increased that a change of quarters also became imperative, and a removal was made from the Browne Block to the second floor of the wooden building, No. 10½ Lafayette street. A Hoe cylinder press was substituted for the little job press, but, proving unsatisfactory, it was exchanged for a Whitlock drum cylinder. This latter machine sufficed the paper was enlarged to 16 x 21 inches. Soon after the office was moved back to the Browne Block, where the enterprise was started. The policy of The News, which was stated to be " the truthful and plain-spoken advocacy of the interests of the citizens of Salem, and to furnish a reliable record of all the fresh news in the vicinity," met with public approval. A strict adherence to this policy has won for The News its present proud position, with a daily circulation of over 16,000, and moreover will enable it to attain to still greater distinction in the future.

A GROUP OF REPRESENTATIVES OF THE SALEM EVENING NEWS.

Upward and onward was the steady advance, and gradually the demand for more room increased, until the proprietor was compelled by urgent necessity to seek larger quarters, where adequate facilities could be commanded for meeting the great demand constantly being made by the public. After exhausting every expedient, a change was made to the new Peabody building, the present location, and on March 28, 1892, a sixteen page souvenir edition was issued. The change meant more than a mere removal. It told of a change of everything connected with or used in the mechanical department—new type, new press and new furniture throughout the establishment, marking an epoch in local journalism which had not entered into the most roseate dreams of the proprietor when he launched The News upon the journalistic sea of toil and trouble. Great, however, as was this change, it came none too soon, and even the new location did not afford spare room. During its seventeen years of existence, The News has kept faith with the public, and its efforts have been appreciated. The little daily which addressed the community on Saturday, October 16, 1880, has become the largest and best penny paper published in New England outside of Boston. In this broad field, the parallel to its achievements can be found only in its own career. During the life of The News there have been a dozen attempts to establish other dailies in Salem, but the opposition has been repeatedly discomfited. The futility has been emphasized again and again of those plans which look to division of a field where public favor, in return for steadfast service, has conspicuously been showered upon the favorite, the recognized medium. Throughout the history of seventeen years of effort, there has been much to promote feelings of pride, but nothing has brought a greater degree of satisfaction than the knowledge that the standard set in the beginning has never passed from sight. Success has been won by the closest adherence to the undeviating policy of being a faithful servant of the people, an impartial herald of current events, an ally to those who have sought the public welfare, a fearless and faithful supporter of every good work having in view the advancement of the interests of the city, and an unflinching advocate of what is believed to be the right, " ever anchoring to principle, rather than trimming its sails to catch the varying breezes, the while idle clamor masquerades as public opinion."

A sketch of The News would be incomplete without mentioning the personality of the active workers, and, therefore, the following brief biographical notices are published :

Robin Damon, the proprietor of The News, was born in North Reading, this state, in September, 1862. He removed with his parents to Middleton when ten years of age, and in that town published a monthly local paper during 1876. In the winter of 1877 he came to Salem, and opened a job printing office in the Browne block, Essex street, remaining there until after The News was some months old. Mr. Damon is married and resides on Lafayette street. He has been a director of the Salem Co-operative bank since it was established, a director of the Salem Board of Trade and Salem Building Association, but has never aspired to public office.

Benj. F. Arrington, who has filled the editorial chair of The News since 1881— the only break in continuous service occurring in 1883-84, when for 13 months he was editor and general manager of a daily paper in Springfield, Mass.,—was born in Leominster, this state, in 1856. He is a practical printer, having learned his trade in the Lynn Reporter office, of which he subsequently became foreman. For nearly two years he served as business manager of the Lynn Daily Bee, at the end of which period he resigned, following the tragic death of its founder, to become the editor of The News. He is a member of several secret societies, and is a past master of Mount Carmel lodge of Masons of Lynn, of which city he has been resident since 1859.

Frank C. Damon, the regular city editor of The News, has been connected with the paper since its birth in 1880, when he commenced as Danvers correspondent and agent. He was born in Middleton, this state, in December, 1865, but, with

EDITOR'S ROOM, SALEM EVENING NEWS.

REPORTERS ROOM, SALEM EVENING NEWS.

his parents, took up his residence in Danvers when yet quite young, receiving his education in the public schools of that town. He is deeply interested in the militia, and spent some ten years in the service, first with the 2nd Corps of Cadets and later with the Eighth Regiment, M. V. M., having been captain of Co. K, and later a major, in the latter organization. He was a selectman of Danvers in 1894. He is a 32d degree Mason and a past master of Amity lodge of Danvers. He is a past noble grand of Danvers lodge of Odd Fellows, and a member of the A. O. one of the original members of the Oxford Musical club, and has composed and published several songs, which have met with a ready sale.

Lorenzo P. Washburn, who holds down the night desk, was born in Natick, Mass., Nov. 5, 1869. He received his education in the public schools of that town and the Cony High school of Augusta, Me. Coming to Salem in 1887, he was for five years the advertiser for Almy, Bigelow & Washburn, and entered the employ of The News in 1892. He is a Knight Templar and a Shriner.

COMPOSING ROOM, SALEM EVENING NEWS.

U. W. He is also a member of the Salem club. He is married and lives with his wife and two children on Washington Sq.

William F. Searle, acting city editor of The News, is a native of Akron, Ohio, and is 31 years of age. He was educated in the public schools of Salem, and has been on the staff of The News for about twelve years, with the exception of brief intervals when absent from the city in other lines of business. He is an authority for this vicinity on sporting matters, and thoroughly conversant with all the departments of newspaper work. He was

Frank Poeton has been on the reportorial staff of The News since June 1, 1896. Mr. Poeton was born April 10, 1871, in Coventry, England, where he received his education, and learned the trade of printer. He came to this country when 17 years of age, and has since been connected with newspaper offices in Connecticut and Massachusetts in the capacities of compositor, proof-reader, foreman and reporter.

Winfield S. Nevins was born in Brunswick, Maine, Dec. 6, 1850, and educated in the schools of New Gloucester, and at

Gorham seminary, Me. He became the Salem district correspondent of the Boston Herald in October, 1873, and has remained in that position during the 24 years. Since Dec., 1895, he has been connected with The News staff. Mr. Nevins served eleven years on the Salem school board, three of them as president. He is a Mason, Odd Fellow, Red Man, member of the Essex Institute and other organizations, and is a past grand master of the Grand Lodge of Odd Fellows of Massachusetts. He is the author of "Witchcraft in Salem Village," "Intervale, N. H.," and "North Shore," and joint author of "Old Naumkeag."

Hugh F. E. Farrell was born in Salem, Jan. 5, 1856, and has ever been a resident of his native city. Instructed in the St. James and Hacker schools, he engaged in the morocco and carriagesmith trades until about 10 years ago when he began corresponding for several Catholic weeklies, and later was employed on the Boston Post, Globe, Fitchburg Mail and other dailies. In January of the present year he joined the reportorial staff of The News.

William H. Damon was born in Danvers, Sept. 14, 1873, and received his education in the public schools of that town. He entered the employ of The News in January, 1896. He is on the reportorial staff.

Harry E. Webber was born in Salem, Feb. 20, 1873. He was educated in the public schools and at the Salem Commercial school. He entered the employ of The News April 23, 1894. His special department is the military, in which he takes great interest, being an honorary member of the Second Corps of Cadets.

STEREOTYPING ROOM, SALEM EVENING NEWS.

Henry C. Gauss, the advertising representative of The News, is a native of Salem, born Nov. 29, 1867. He entered the employ of The News shortly after graduating from the Salem High School, and served a reportorial apprenticeship. He left The News to manage the second Salem Telegram, going subsequently to the Boston Record. Mr. Gauss has been connected with several Massachusetts suburban dailies and for three years was managing editor of the Oil City, Pa., Derrick. In 1895 Mr. Gauss was appointed special Boston advertising representative of The News and shortly after was called to the local field. Mr. Gauss has had an all-round experience in newspaper work on both large and small papers, and is equally at home in the business office and the editorial room. Mr. Gauss is married and resides on Boardman street.

Harry E. Flint was born in Middleton, Jan. 23, 1874, and received his education in the public schools of Salem. He entered the employ of The News in May 1890, in the business office.

The mechanical department of The News is presided over by the following:

John B. Tivnan is in the composing room. He has been with the paper ever since it started, in various capacities, rising from newsboy to his present position. Mr. Tivnan was born in Lynn in 1868. He was educated in Salem's schools, and has always been identified with the city's interests. He is a member of the overseers of the poor. Mr. Tivnan is married and lives on Hancock street.

Richard M. Hiller, foreman of the stereotyping department, has been in the office nearly seven years, coming here when the new plant was established. He is a veteran in his line.

Frederick N. Cole, the foreman of the press-room, is an old timer on The News, having been with the office over a dozen years. He was born in 1852, and now resides in Salem with his family.

The late George W. Parsons was an esteemed employee of The News. He was probably the oldest working printer in the state at the time of his death. Mr. Parsons was born in Newburyport in 1815, and had always followed the printing business in various positions. He was in The News' composing room nearly seventeen years, and his faithful services will long be remembered.

PRESS ROOM, SALEM EVENING NEWS.

Hon. William H. Moody.

Upon the death of the lamented Gen. Cogswell in the early spring of 1895, the republican thought of the old Essex district turned instinctively to Hon. William H. Moody of Haverhill, at that time serving his fifth year as district attorney for the eastern district of Massachusetts, as his successor. He is a native of Newbury, where he was born Dec. 23, 1853. He graduated from Phillips Academy, Andover, in 1872, and from Harvard University four years later. Devoting himself to the study of law, Mr. Moody has since practiced in Haverhill with marked success

Gen. Cogswell, receiving 15,064 votes to 5,815 for Hon. H. N. Shepard of Boston, democrat. One year later, Mr. Moody was re-elected by a majority of some 12,000 over Hon. E. M. Boynton of West Newbury. The sixth congressional district is hot and bursty, comprising, as it

HON. W. H. MOODY CONGRESSMAN 6TH DISTRICT

and has acted as city solicitor. His incumbency of the district attorneyship was a most notable one, and attracted wide attention. At a special election held at the time of the regular state election in November, 1895, he was elected to succeed

does the major portion of Essex county, with a population, according to the United States census of 1890, of 160,418. Of the many and diversified interests there involved, Mr. Moody has been a most acceptable representative. In the fifty

fourth congress he served on the com- speaker and his eulogy upon Gen. Cogs-
mittee upon expenditures in the depart- well, delivered in congress on the day set
ment of justice and election committee apart for such memorials, was one of the
No. 1. His work upon the vexatious best heard there in recent years. Mr.
problems arising from contested election Moody is prominent in social life in his
cases which this committee was called home city and is a member of leading
upon to consider, was eminently fair to social and business organizations.

HON. W. S. KNOX CONGRESSMAN 5TH DISTRICT.

by Mr. Knox is considered to have the greatest textile interests of any district in the country, including such manufacturing centres as Lawrence and Lowell. Not for a moment was there a doubt that the interests of the fifth district would be amply protected by its present congressman and these anticipations have been abundantly justified. The subject of our sketch was born in Killingly, Conn., Sept. 10, 1843, moved to Lawrence when nine years of age, and has resided in that city ever since. He graduated from Amherst college in 1865 and in the fall of the following year was admitted to the Essex bar. The legal practice of Mr. Knox has always been a large one and he was chosen city solicitor in 1875-6, and again in 1887-8-9-90. In 1874-5 he was a member of the Massachusetts house of representatives, his legal acumen placing him upon the judiciary committee. He has been markedly successful in business movements and is now president of the Arlington National Bank of Lawrence. Mr. Knox opposed Hon. Moses T. Stevens in 1892, for a seat in the fifty-third congress, but was defeated by a narrow margin. In 1894, however, he won by a good majority over Hon. George W. Fifield, democrat, and in the republican tidal wave of November, 1896, he was given 17,835 votes to 11,531 for Hon. J. H. Harrington of Lowell, his democratic opponent. In the fifty-fourth congress, Mr. Knox served upon the committees on territories and expenditures upon public buildings. Upon the questions arising from reports by these committees, he spoke frequently and with effect. Perhaps the most important of the bills which he presented was that providing for a uniform system of bankruptcy. Bankruptcy legislation was a subject of particular interest to Mr. Knox, other speeches dealing with the proposed international monetary conference and various territorial matters. In the recent special session of congress, the opinion of the member from the fifth Massachusetts district was most weighty in the consideration of the economic problems there presented for solution. Mr. Knox's views are in line with those of the republican majority. Personally he is most affable and numbers friends by legions.

Nicholas M. Quint.

One of the most popular members of the legislature of recent years is Nicholas M. Quint of Peabody, who for several terms past represented the tenth, formerly the twenty-first Essex district in the lower house. Mr. Quint is not a native of Peabody, but in his long residence there he has become a vital part of the town life and is among its most substantial citizens. He was born in Eaton, N. H., July 18, 1838. The family was an old one in that section and Mr. Quint's father was a member of the New Hampshire legislature at the time of his death. The subject of this sketch was educated at Fryeburg (Me.) Academy and after his graduation removed to Peabody. Responding to the Union call, he enlisted in Company C of the Fifth Massachusetts, July 21, 1863, and served one year, participating in the battles of Kingston, Whitehall, Blount's Creek, Gouldsboro, and other affairs in North Carolina. Since 1864, Mr. Quint has been largely interested in real estate matters. His judgment in all phases of this business is considered of the very best and to his credit may be placed the development of a large section of the town. He is also a contractor and gives employment to a large force of men. By his business sagacity and foresight, Mr. Quint has acquired a competence, but is still active in commercial life and is among the heaviest taxpayers in the town. By his broad real estate knowledge, he was called upon to serve as an assessor in 1885-6-7; he was a water commissioner in 1886 and superintendent of the water system for six years, beginning in 1888. In 1895 he became chairman of the park commissioners. Mr. Quint's first experience in state law making was in 1894 and he served continuously as a member of the house until 1898. The value of the counsel of the member from Peabody was recognized from the first and his committee work was of the best. During his first term he served upon the committee on water supply and was chairman of the same the following year. Mr. Quint was also a member of the committees on liquor law and roads and bridges. His entire legislative career has been most acceptable to his constituents who are not backward in expressing their appreciation of the same. Mr. Quint is prominent in secret society life, being a member of Jordan lodge, F. & A. M., Holten lodge, I. O. O. F., and Masconomo tribe of Red Men. He takes an active interest in the Grand Army and is a past commander of Union post, 50, of Peabody. In his long and extensive real estate movements, Mr. Quint has assisted many of moderate circumstances to become owners of homes and is now a leader in the worthy efforts of the Peabody Co-operative Bank, acting as a director and a member of the security committee. He also belongs to the Board of Trade. He is an ardent republican and is considered to bear a striking facial resemblance to Senator Mark Hanna of Ohio and on the occasion of

NICHOLAS M. QUINT.

a recent visit to the national capital was accosted by one who mistook him for the noted political manager. As a self-made man, Mr. Quint abundantly deserves the eminence which he now enjoys.

Hon. James H. Turner.

Hon. James H. Turner in 1897 served his fourth term as chief executive of the city of Salem, his vote increasing at each election. He was a member of the board of aldermen in '90, '91, '92 and '93, receiving the largest vote of any candidate, and was at one time tendered the chairmanship of the board, but declined. Mayor Turner has spent his entire life in this city, and his occupation has always been that of a leather measurer. He is a war veteran and a respected member of Post 34, G. A. R. He also belongs to John Endicott lodge, A. O. U. W., Niagara council, O. U. A. M., Salem Veteran Firemen, Fraternity lodge, I. O. O. F., Sheridan club, and other organizations. To Mayor Turner's extended connection with municipal affairs, many public improvements and conveniences are largely due. By his generous and affable disposition, he attracts to himself men of all parties and no party, and in no way does he violate their confidence. The satisfying of his own conscience is the criterion upon which he measures public problems. Such an administration of municipal affairs, the citizens of Salem obviously appreciate. Mr. Turner is considered an expert in his line of busi-

HON. JAMES H. TURNER.

ness and has always had large employment. He is a republican, a heavy real estate owner, and resides at 69 Boston street.

Joseph Hardy Phippen.

Having passed four score and ten, Joseph Hardy Phippen is one of the oldest citizens of Salem. Moreover, having spent his entire life in this city and for more than half a century actively identified with its best interests, no history of Salem would be complete without some reference to the work of this venerable man. Mr. Phippen was born on Hardy street, June 10, 1807. He was the son of Hardy and Ursula (Symonds) Phippen, his father being one of the leading mariners then sailing from this port. Joseph was first sent to a private school, then attended the East school on Forrester street, Master Gerrish in charge. His father returned from a voyage at this time and transferred him to William Carne's private school on Sewall street, the son's education being completed at the then new building in South Salem, under Master Gale. Captain Phippen

JOSEPH HARDY PHIPPEN.

soon after retired from voyaging and started in the grocery business, the subject of this sketch being associated with him in the store. The work was not to the liking of the younger man and he applied for and secured a clerkship in the post office under Postmaster Joseph E. Sprague. While in this position he cast his first vote—for John Quincy Adams in his unsuccessful campaign against Andrew Jackson. Mr. Phippen has always been deeply interested in public affairs and an election of any kind brings him to the polls. October 20, 1828, began what was

He identified himself with the Tabernacle church in 1858, and has served as treasurer and deacon. In March, 1840, he married Miss Susan H. Lord, who died February 3, 1882. November 26, 1883, he married Miss Emma Lord. Despite his advanced age, Mr. Phippen takes a great interest in the city and still makes frequent visits to the scenes of his former activity.

Hon. John D. H. Gauss.

Hon. John D. H. Gauss, who represents

HON. JOHN D. H. GAUSS AND HIS LITTLE GIRLS.

destined to be his life work. On that date he entered the Mercantile Bank as a clerk and so continued until June, 1852, when he was promoted to cashier, succeeding the late Stephen Webb. For over forty years he held this position, resigning March 7, 1893, making his connection with the bank extend over a period of nearly sixty-five years. Mr. Phippen served upon the school committee before the establishment of the city government and during the administration of several of the earlier mayors.

the 2d Essex district in the Massachusetts senate, was born in Salem, Jan. 4th, 1861, and has always lived here. His father was Stephen Gauss, a well-known and substantial citizen of that portion of the city known as "Down Town" and his mother was Rebecca Gray (Cross) Gauss, one of the teachers of the old East or Phillips school. It was there, at the old Phillips, that the senator received his early education, but at the completion of the prescribed course he went to old Master Leavitt, a famous private tutor for many years, for a special course in book-keeping and commercial arithmetic. In November of the same year, 1875, Mr. Gauss entered the Salem Observer office, as boy in the press room, and has been connected with the office, as boy and man ever since, the firm being now Newcomb & Gauss, who are the printers of this book, the senior partner being George F. Newcomb. Mr. Gauss has been, for six years, a member of the Salem school committee, his most important work therewith being the introduction of the kindergarten in connection with the public school course. In 1893, the people of the 15th Essex representative district sent him to the legislature, where he served three years in the house of representatives and then was advanced to the upper branch. It is scarcely necessary therefore to say that Mr. Gauss is an ardent republican, the president of the Young Men's Republican club, and a member of other political organizations. He has also been connected with the secret societies, including the Masons and the Odd Fellows, holding high position in the latter order. Mr. Gauss is married and has an interesting family of four children.

Late Jabez B. Lyman, M. D.

J. B. Lyman, A. M., M. D., came to Salem in 1880, and from that time until his death, resided at 92 Washington square in the old Baldwin homestead. Dr. Lyman was a nephew of the late Jabez Baldwin, the founder of the Boston firm of Shreve, Crump & Low. Dr. Lyman was born in Easthampton, Mass., April 18, 1820, his father being Ahira Lyman, his mother, Lydia Baldwin. His father and mother died when he was yet a youth. He was educated at Amherst college, from which institution he was graduated in 1841. After graduating from college, he went abroad spending four years in study and travel, much of the time in the universities of Halle and Berlin, under Tholuck and Neander. Returning to this country, he was connected for some time as instructor of French and German with Amherst college. In 1850, he was made professor of mathematics in Oglethorpe University, (Ga.) In 1853 he returned to Europe, where he began the study of medicine in Paris, Berlin, and other medical centres. Returning to this country, he received his medical degree from Jefferson Medical college (Phil. del-

LATE JABEZ B. LYMAN, M. D.

phia), and shortly afterwards established himself in his profession in Rockford, Illinois, where he attained a prominent position as surgeon and oculist, being recognized as an able practitioner throughout the state. At the close of the war of the rebellion he received the appointment of United States pension surgeon, which position he held for over twenty years. During his long residence in Rockford, he took a very prominent part in educational work, being identified in an official capacity with all the educational institutions of the city. He was one of the founders of the Rockford free public library, and the Y. M. C. A. He was a frequent lecturer before the Rockford college, and contributor to literary and scientific journals both abroad and in this country, his long residence in Europe giving him complete mastery of the French and German languages. He was also a lover and patron of art. Upon the death of the surviving member of the Baldwin family, he determined to make Salem his home, coming here in 1880, where he resided until his death in 1893. Dr. Lyman was a man of broad and accurate scholarship, keeping abreast of the latest and most useful discoveries in the line of his profession, a man of high culture, noble purposes, and kindly disposition. Dr. Lyman married Sept. 5, 1860, Lucy De Pue, daughter of Ephraim DePue and Maria Dennis of Galesburg, Illinois. She survives him, with five of their eight children.

Col. Henry A. Hale.

Col. Henry Appleton Hale is descended from among the earliest settlers of this section, his grandfather on his father's side coming to Salem from Newbury in 1801 was a charter member of the Salem Light Infantry in 1805, and was a successful merchant in the Mediterranean trade until his death. He is also a descendant of Major Samuel Appleton, a pioneer of the town of Ipswich, and commander of the Massachusetts forces during the early colonial wars. Col. Hale's father was a successful business man of this city, engaging in the hardware trade from 1828 until the time of his death in 1890, and was the builder of the Hale block. The subject of this sketch was born in Salem and is a graduate of the public and high schools. He left with the first company of the Salem Light Infantry

COL. HENRY A. HALE, PRESIDENT SALEM GAS LIGHT CO.

for the front in 1861, his original enlistment being for three months. Up to the time of his final discharge, November 11, 1865, Mr. Hale rose through the various grades of private, lieutenant, captain, brigade inspector, assistant adjutant-general, with the brevet of lieutenant-colonel connected with the staff of General Ruger of the twenty-third army corps. Throughout his entire service Col. Hale was conspicuous for courage, and was wounded at Antietam and Cold Harbor. Returning to the more peaceful pursuits of life, Col. Hale associated with his father in the hardware business, and after the latter's death continued until 1896, when he disposed of the business. He has been president of the Salem Gas Light Company for five years and for a much longer period has been a director in the same enterprise. In rooms adjacent to the office of the gas company, Col. Hale does a large business in the most approved appliances for gas lighting and heating. He is one of the vice presidents of the Salem Five Cents Savings Bank and a member of the investment committee. He belongs to the Salem club, Veteran Light Infantry Association, Ancient and Honorable Artillery Association, Society of Colonial Wars, and of the Military Order of the Loyal Legion, an organization composed entirely of officers in the late war. He has recently retired from an extended service upon the board of park commissioners. Col. Hale is a typical Salemite of the most substantial type, and his name has become synonomous with unswerving integrity in the various walks of a busy life.

William H. Jelly.

William H. Jelly, president of the Salem Five Cents Savings Bank, is a native of Salem, and the son of the late William Jelly, who for some time was superintendent of the Salem Water Works, and was a resident of the city as early as 1795. The subject of this sketch was born November 12, 1820, and was educated in the public schools. At the age of 14 he left school and entered the post office as a general utility boy, remaining there five years and receiving several promotions. In 1839 he yielded to his inclination for a sea-faring life and made several trips to the Antipodes, Zanzibar, and other foreign ports. These voyages were made in trading vessels, whose missions proved very successful. Mr. Jelly finally settled in Zanzibar with the purpose of engaging in trade. He so continued for eight years, and the venture was a happy one, Mr. Jelly later returning to his native city. He has since been a leader in the commercial life of Salem, connected for many years with the institution of which he is now the head. He was for many years president

WILLIAM H. JELLY, PRES. FIVE CENTS SAVINGS BANK.

of the Salem Gas Light Co. He has taken
an active interest in public affairs, serving for eight years as an overseer of the
poor, has also been upon the school board,
a trustee of both the Old Men's and Old
Ladies' homes, trustee Plummer Farm
school, and was one of the incorporators

J. Clifford Entwisle.

J. Clifford Entwisle, city clerk of Salem, was born in Brooklyn, June 17, 1852,
and attended the public schools of New
York and the College of the City of New
York. At the age of 15, he made his

J. CLIFFORD ENTWISLE, City Clerk.

of the Salem Hospital. Mr. Jelly is
known throughout the entire community
for his numerous acts of charity, public
spiritedness, and interest in the general
welfare of his fellowmen, who have been
pleased in honoring him in public
trusts.

first voyage to sea in the famous emigrant
ship, William Tapscott. In 1872, he
shipped before the mast on the tea clip-
per Surprise, belonging to the late Abiel
A. Low, formerly of Salem. He continued in the China, Japan, Australia and
East India trade for the next twenty

years, sailing as third and second mate of the Surprise until she was wrecked in Yeddo Bay, about 18 miles from Yokohama, in February, 1876. The ship was under the command of the late Capt. Frederick Johnson, and in charge of a pilot. In the fall of the same year, Capt. Entwisle joined the ship Sacramento of Boston at San Francisco, commanded by the late Capt. William H. Nelson of Salem, as second mate, afterwards serving as chief mate for five years. He assumed command of the Sacramento in 1882; after a successful voyage to China and return, Capt. Entwisle was transferred to the ship Ringleader of Boston, belonging to the same owners. This ship he commanded for seven years, making his last trip in 1891. He was a member of the common council for three years, serving as president in 1894. The next year he was chosen an alderman and is now in his second term as city clerk. Capt. Entwisle is a member of many organizations, among the number being the Masons, A. O. U. W., Honorary Cadets, Congregational club, Salem and Boston Marine societies, Honorary G. A. R., Cogswell and Colonial clubs, K. A. E. O., and Salem Board of Trade. He resides on Linden street.

Henry W. Peabody.

Henry W. Peabody was born in Salem, August 22, 1838, and has always resided here except during four years of his childhood, between one and five years of age, at Montevideo and Buenos Ayres, where his father, Alfred Peabody, was then engaged in business. His ancestry on the paternal side includes Alfred, 1804, Nathan, 1770, Moses, 1743, John, 1714, David, 1678, and Lieut. Francis John, 1642. The maternal (Travis) line includes George, 1795, Thomas, 1762, and David, 1724. He was educated in the public schools of Salem and the private school of Master Worcester and left the Latin school to enter the counting room of Williams & Hall, China and India merchants, on Central wharf, Boston, January 1, 1856. In 1859 he assumed a responsible clerkship with Samuel Stevens, engaged in the Australian trade. This business increased and ex-

HENRY W. PEABODY.

SUMMER RESIDENCE OF HENRY W. PEABODY AT BEVERLY.

tended to other foreign countries, and in 1862 Mr. Peabody became a partner in the firm of Samuel Stevens & Co. A large business was developed with India, Africa and Australia and some fine ships for freighting were built. In 1866 Mr. Peabody retired, as the depreciation of property in merchandise and vessels had occasioned loss of the gains of the previous years. He renewed his efforts under a special partnership in his own name in February, 1867, and has continued to this day as senior partner in the firm of Henry W. Peabody & Co., in progressive business with many foreign countries. The Australian freighting, once of great importance to Boston, was necessarily transferred about seven years ago to New York, where his partners reside. The Boston house continues business, principally importations of hemp from Yucatan, where they have their own house, and Manilla, where they are in connection with a leading English firm. They also have offices at London and Sydney, N. S. W., and correspondents in many parts of the world. The daily attendance of Mr. Peabody to his business in Boston, and his frequent trips to New York and occasionally to London and twice to Australia, have not allowed of his taking active part in city affairs, except in efforts to secure good government. He was a member of the Law and Order League during its existence. In the last few years he has taken a deep interest in the currency question in defense of the gold standard, and has been a republican in politics. He has always attended the First Baptist church of which he has been a member since 1866, is now a member of the society committee, deacon of the church, and was superintendent of the Sunday School for two years. He is director and was formerly vice-president of the Young Men's Christian Association. His residence in Salem is not continuous, as his family spend a long season at his summer home at Montserrat, Beverly, where he also has considerable interest in a syndicate for the development of some beautiful country into convenient building sites for residences. His Salem home, since 1864, is at 19 Chestnut street.

LATE EDWARD F. BALCH.

Late Edward F. Balch.

Edward Frank Balch, son of Capt. Benjamin Balch, was born in Salem, Nov.

27, 1842. He received his education in the public schools and under Master John F. Worcester, a former well known private instructor. Mr. Balch entered the employ of a Boston firm, in whose office he remained for some years. For the same concern he afterwards went to New York, but later returned to his native city and began as an apprentice to learn the trade of a machinist at the Salem machine shops. He so served for three years, was moved to second hand and finally became superintendent. In this position he soon became popular and prominent among his business associates. He developed a wide knowledge of the business, while his sound judgment and uniform courtesy made him welcome in both business and social circles. Some years later, Mr. Balch went to C____ where he managed the milling affairs of the Pacific Manufacturing Company. He returned to Salem soon after to accept a responsible position at the Naumkeag mills, and in 1878 he was called to become agent of the mills, where, only seven years before, he had served his first apprenticeship. To the Naumkeag corporation, as to every enterprise with which he was concerned, he brought a remarkable capacity, coupled with untiring energy and perseverance, making success a certainty. Mr. Balch died at his summer home in Wenham, August 20, 1897. His wife, Elizabeth S. (Perkins), whom he married June 5, 1873, with two daughters and one son survive him.

Late Nathan R. Morse, A. M., M. D.

Nathan Ransom Morse, A. M., M. D., one of the most prominent physicians of recent years residing in this city, was born at Stoddard, N. H., Feb. 20, 1834. He was the oldest of a family of eight children, three of the four sons devoting themselves to the study of the healing art. Dr. Morse was descended from Samuel Morse, the distinguished Puritan who emigrated from England to the new world in 1635. The subject of this sketch entered Amherst college in 1855, and graduated four years later. During his college course he was interested largely in geological work. He studied for a time at the Harvard Medical school, but completed his professional preparation at the University of Vermont, from which he graduated in June, 1862. After practicing for three years in the town of

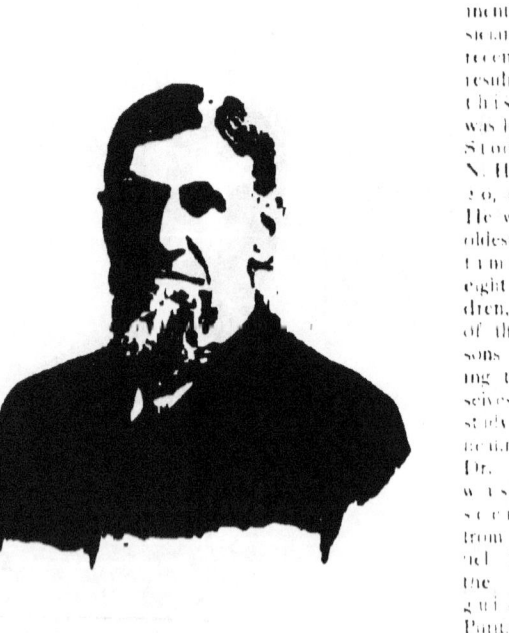

LATE NATHAN R. MORSE, A. M., M. D.

Reading, Dr. Morse settled in Salem, remaining till the time of his death. His acquired reputation as a physician was an enviable one and his services were often called upon outside of his immediate practice. He was one of the founders of the medical department of Boston University, subscribing $1,000 towards this object. In the Boston institution he was professor of the diseases of women and children from 1874 to 1879. Dr. Morse was secretary of the Massachusetts Homœopathic Medical Society in 1878-9, edited volumes IV and V of the society's transactions and was its orator in 1874. He was secretary of the Essex County Homœopathic Medical Society from 1872 to 1879, and later its president; was also president of the Massachusetts Surgical and Gynaecological Society, and senior member of the American Institute of Homœopathy. In the latter organization, Dr. Morse made the motion to admit women to the membership, it being, in consequence, the first medical society in which women were eligible. In 1866 he was made a Master Mason in Essex lodge of this city. A few years later he joined the Odd Fellows and was also a charter member of North Star lodge, K. of P. By disease and accident, Dr. Morse was incapacitated from his duties in 1880. Seeking the quiet of Baker's island, his recovery to health was most rapid, and to the trained mind of the physician came the natural suggestion to make of the island a comfortable and home-like health resort. In 1887 he purchased the property and began the enlargement of the old farm house, which at that time was the only building on the island outside of the government reservation. More substantial additions have since been made, until the Winne-Egan can furnish ample accommodations for one hundred guests, and Baker's island, dotted with beautiful cottages, is coming to be regarded as one of the finest resorts on the New England coast. Dr. Morse was married in 1859 to Miss Lottie L. Barden of Marion. She died in 1862, leaving two sons, Frederick L. and William. In 1864 he married Miss Rebecca H. Brown of Bernardston, and by this marriage had three sons and one daughter, the oldest son, Charles W. Morse, being a physician and surgeon of large practice in Salem, spending the winter of 1893-4 in Vienna for the purpose of study. The second son, George A., is a graduate of Amherst college and of Harvard Law school, and is acting as private secretary to Presiding Justice Goodrich of the New York supreme court. Henry W. Morse, the youngest son, has studied at the scientific department of Harvard University, but is now proprietor and manager of the Winne-Egan. Dr. Morse was a man of acute and vigorous intellect and rugged strength of character. He was positive in his opinions and resolute in maintaining them, but of a genial, kindly and sympathetic nature. No worthy application for assistance went unheeded with him, and with the skill of the physician were mingled the kindly offices of the personal friend. In this capacity few have excelled him. In every circle where he moved throughout his busy life, he was the central figure — a strong bond of union, the loss of which will only be more keenly felt as time rolls on.

LATE NATHANIEL ROPES.

Late Nathaniel Ropes.

A quiet and retired life, filled with innumerable kindnesses and charitable acts, was that of Nathaniel Ropes, who died in this city, February 6, 1893. Mr. Ropes was an Ohioan by birth, and received a common school education. He prepared for Harvard College, graduating with abundant honor in 1855. His school days over, Mr. Ropes returned to his home in Cincinnati, there engaging in business with his father. Ten years after, he settled in Salem, acting as agent for his aunt, Mrs. Sarah F. Orne, in the care of her extensive estate, becoming heir to the same at her death. In politics, Mr. Ropes was a democrat, but never aspired to public position. He was a member of the Ohio National Guard. By his thorough knowledge of business methods and his integrity he commanded the esteem of all. With wholesome discrimination, he was markedly generous, giving not from impulse but from a sense of duty.

William F. Cass.

Soon after the second inauguration of President Cleveland, a change in the Salem postmastership became in order, and, as it seemed, by general consent the honor was conferred upon William F. Cass, one of the best known and highly esteemed of the younger business men of the city. Mr. Cass's entire life has been spent here, having been born in North Salem thirty-six years ago. He attended the North primary and Pickering schools, and at an early age his mercantile training began in the shoe stock business. Later he changed to the motor conductors industry, serving his time at the trade, and conducting business on his own account in Peabody and in this city. Mr. Cass closed

Respectfully
William F. Cass.

out his private interests upon assuming the postmastership in December, 1893. At that time he was about to conclude his second year in the board of aldermen, and had previously received four successive elections to the common council, representing Ward 4 as a democrat. Mr.

SALEM 1626-1897

Cass has been known as an active temperance worker, serving two terms as president of the Young Men's Catholic Temperance society. He was chairman of the committee having in charge the erection of the Father Mathew monument, and at the dedicatory exercises officially transferred the memorial to the care of the city. He is a trustee of the Veragua council, Knights of Columbus. He is married, has two children and resides at 150 Boston street. Mr. Cass's administration of postal affairs has been most efficient. Some two years ago, following an extensive enlargement and refitting, association known as the Post Office block, at 118 Washington street. Of recent years, and especially during the term of Postmaster William F. Cass, the mail facilities have been greatly increased and extended. Ten mails are received from, and the same number sent to Boston each week day, with equally good service to nearer and more remote points. In the city are eighty-eight mail boxes, from which frequent collections are made during the day and early evening. A delivery is made in the business section at 7.30 A. M., and full deliveries at 8.30 A. M., 1.15 and 4.15 P. M. On week days the office

SALEM POST OFFICE EMPLOYEES.

Thos. F. Sheehan, Jas. J. Cahill, Geo. L. Cooke, M. J. O'Keefe, C. F. Kingsley, John F. Coyne, J. M. Coynes, Lewis F. Brown, Walter H. Hall, Chas. W. Gardner, S. A. Ferguson, Wm. H. Morgan, G. W. Whipple, J. F. Prescott, Richard B. Reed, H. P. Nourse, Geo. W. H. Brown, P. A. Pelletier, Jas. Manning, Jas. W. Nichols, Hos. Bartmeby, Chas. W. Gardner, V. F. Pepper, W. M. Perkins, Fred P. Willard, Wm. F. Cass, F. F. Campbell.

the office was badly damaged by fire and water, but the immense quantity of matter which was being handled at the time, suffered little or no delay, the achievement being a most notable one in the face of the handicapping caused by the fire. The facilities and service have been improved in every possible way, and the Salem postoffice is in the front rank for general efficiency.

Salem Post Office.

The Salem post office is located in the building of the Essex County Building is open from 7 A. M. to 8 P. M., and on Sundays from 11.30 A. M. to 12.30 P. M. During the last four years the receipts increased twenty per cent., and for the last fiscal year aggregated nearly $50,000. The amount involved in the money order department is about $200,000 per annum. From fifty to sixty per cent. of the receipts are used in the running expenses. The names of carriers, number of route and date of original appointment follow: J. Frank Whipple, 1, 1869; Samuel A. Ferguson, 2, 1875; Henry P. Nourse, 3, 1883; George W. H. Brown, 4, 1872, Charles W. Gardner, 5, 1872;

Alfred P. Jacques, 6, 1882; Arthur L. Pepper, 7, 1884; Richard B. Reed, 8, 1855; Charles W. Getchell, (Superintendent), 9, 1885; Caleb F. Kingsley, 10, 1888; William H. Morgan, 11, 1890 James W. Nichols, 12, 1880; Thomas Darmody, 13, 1888; Louis F. Brown, 14, 1889; Walter M. Perkins, 15, 1889; Peter A. Pelletier, 16, 1892. Mr. Reed began as a penny post in 1855, and claims to have the longest continuous service in mail delivery of any man now in the employ of the government. The substitute carriers, with date of appointment are Matthias J. O'Keefe, 1894; James J. Carian, 1894; John L. Currie, 1895; George W. Curtis, 1896. The office clerks, with department and date of appointment are George F. Cossetians, 1892; Walter H. H... 1893; ... 1897; Thomas M. ..., ... 1885; ... Cass, general delivery, 1894; Thomas F. Sheehan, general delivery, 1889; Charles R. Doyle, stamp ..., 1894; James Manning, ... distribution, 1890. Although now ... eight-h year, Mr. Manning is as active in his duties as ever. Forest L. Prescott, 1897, and Fredie K P Willard, 1897, are special delivery messengers. Postmaster Cass is assisted by G

Willis Whipple, appointed shortly after Mr. Cass assumed charge of the office. With the sanction of the department officials at Washington, the service in Salem could be still more improved, as by the appointment of two additional carriers, and a clerk who should receive and prepare night mails, besides making a collection trip to the principal letter boxes throughout the city. All of which will doubtless come in due time.

DR. WALTER P. BECKWITH.

Salem Normal School.

The normal school system of the Bay state is almost without an equal in that department of instruction. In the front rank of the several institutions of this kind under the state's supervision and ... the subject of this sketch, the school ... the corner of Lafayette street and Loring avenue in the city of Salem. The first class in the history of the school was received in a two-story building on Summer street, September, 1854. Dr. Richard Edwards, the first principal, had an administration of three years. Prof. Alpheus Crosby having charge in the succeeding eight years. Both were thorough educators and the school advanced rapidly, requiring additional accommodations in 1865. In the same year, Dr. Daniel B.

Hagar accepted the principalship, continuing until ill-health caused his resignation early in 1896, followed a short time later by his death. In 1892, upon the recommendation of the board of visitors, $250,000 was appropriated by the legislature for the purchase of a lot and the construction of a suitable building. Land was purchased early in 1893 and in the fall of the same year the building work began. The dedication occurred January 26, 1897, with appropriate exercises and in the presence of leading instructors and officials. The present principal is Dr. Walter P. Beckwith. The total enrollment since the inception of the school has been nearly 4,500, of whom about one-half have regularly graduated. Sixty teachers have been employed. The present building is located in a most commanding position in the southern part of the city. It is of buff brick with light stone trimmings, and has three stories and a basement. The main building is 180 feet in length, with two wings, each 140 feet long. Every convenience is available and the arrangement is of the best. The sanitation, ventilation, heating and lighting apparatus and general equipment leave little to be desired. The attendance is largely from Essex and Middlesex counties, although several states are represented. For admission, a high school education or its equivalent is required. The regular course of study requires two years, but special or partial courses may be taken, as a rule, classes being admitted only at the beginning of the fall term. The faculty numbers twelve persons. Most abundantly has the Salem Normal school fulfilled its mission as conceived at its founding—" of reviving and establishing the normal method of learning, teaching, and living in the older portion of the commonwealth."

Walter P. Beckwith, Ph. D.

In June, 1896, the citizens of the town of Adams learned with regret of the election of their highly esteemed superintendent of schools to the principalship of the Salem Normal school. In his nineteen years' oversight of the education of the youth of the Berkshire town, Mr. Beckwith had become a part of the local life. The sundering of these ties seemed inevitable, as the Salem position was too attractive to be refused. All, however, felt a great measure of pride in the high honor which had been conferred upon their townsman, which has been fully justified during his comparatively brief administration of the state normal school in this city. Mr. Beckwith was chosen to his present position from among a large list of worthy candidates. The school was entering upon a new era, a new building, perhaps the finest of its kind in New England, being about to be dedicated, involving additional duties which the opening of extra departments must of necessity bring about. From the first, the interest of the new principal in the school and in the city has been deep and sincere. Walter P. Beckwith was born at Lempster, N. H., Aug. 27, 1850, of English and Scotch parentage. In early life he had only the limited educational advantages of a youth in a small farming community. He spent three years as a teacher in and about his native town, later attending the Claremont high school for a short time and graduating from the Kimball Union academy at Meriden in 1871. In his college career at Tufts, he was obliged to be absent a portion of the time to assist himself by teaching, one period comprising an entire year. Mr. Beckwith's standing as a student was very high and he graduated with honor. The position of principal of the Chicopee Falls high school was offered and accepted, this relation continuing until January, 1878. Of Mr. Beckwith's service at Adams much could be said. Mr. Beckwith is a thorough educator and to his credit may be put a great portion of the praise for the high standing enjoyed by the schools of that town. During his service the town expended $100,000 in new buildings and the school appropriation had almost trebled. He enjoyed the confidence of the business men of the town to a great degree and in his work he received the most substantial support. During his long residence in Adams he had become identified with many interests aside from his school duties. For thirteen years he served as chairman of the public library trustees,

SALEM 1626-1897

NEW STATE NORMAL SCHOOL.

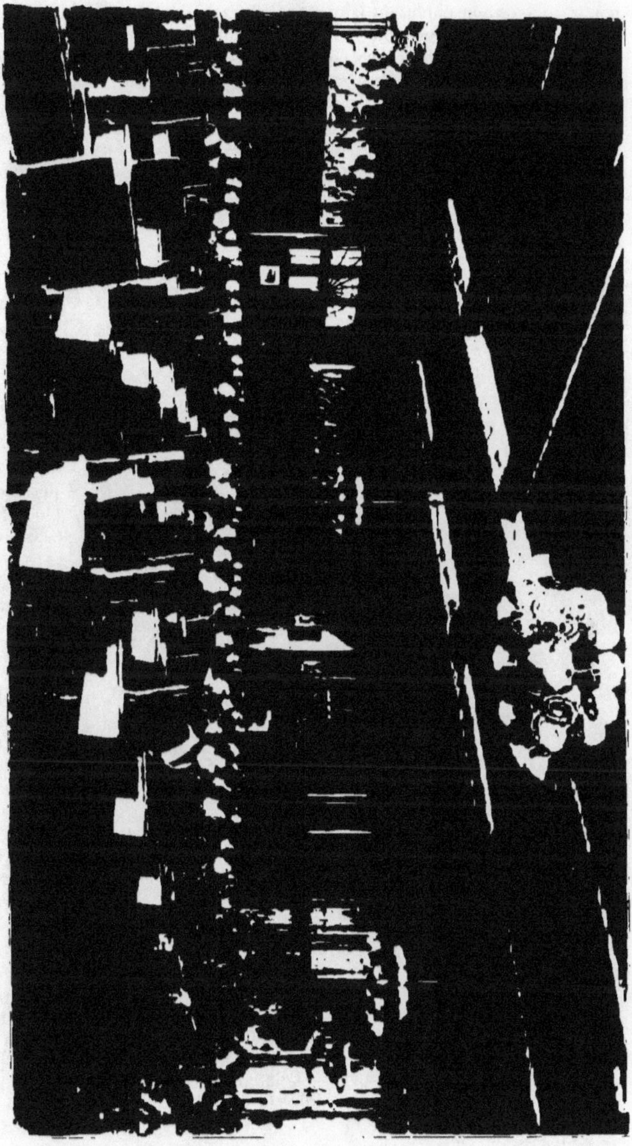

MAIN STUDY HALL, SALEM NORMAL SCHOOL.

was repeatedly elected moderator of town meetings and served upon important committees. Mr. Beckwith attends the Universalist church, is a Mason, member of the A. O. U. W. and of the Tufts College chapter, Phi Beta Kappa. He has written largely to various periodicals and is an effective public speaker. A member of numerous educational societies, he has been honored by the degrees of A. M. and Ph. D. on behalf of his alma mater. December 23, 1870, Mr. Beckwith was united in marriage with Miss Mary I. Sayles, a teacher in the Adams public schools. He has one daughter. Fortunate, indeed, was our state when she drafted to her service in a foremost institution this able educator and thorough man.

Salem Commercial School.

The Salem Commercial school has steadily grown since its foundation, in 1890, from a small class held at the home of Miss E. A. Tibbetts, for several years its principal, until today it occupies more than 5,000 square feet of floor space in the Peabody building on Washington street, in the heart of Salem's business section, within easy reach of steam and electric lines. The entire management of the school is now in the hands of George P. Lord, who

GEORGE P. LORD.

is a native of Salem and a graduate of the Salem high school and also of one of the leading business schools in the state. His first association with the school which he now controls was in 1891, when he became assistant instructor in arithmetic and commercial law, while still pursuing his studies preparatory for admission to the bar. Finding himself well adapted to teaching, he decided to abandon his law studies and, when the school was incorporated, in 1894, he was elected treasurer, becoming assistant principal in 1896 and assuming full charge of the school in March, 1897. Besides Mr. Lord, the faculty is composed of Frank A. Tibbetts, instructor in bookkeeping and business practice, Miss C. I. Carter, assistant instructor in bookkeeping and office practice, Mrs. Emma Smith Lord, instructor in shorthand, Miss Mabel L. Jones, instructor in typewriting by touch, Frank W. Martin, instructor in penmanship. Each member of the faculty was chosen because of special adaptability to the subject in hand and since all are well and favorably known in Salem, it is unnecessary to further dilate upon their qualification for the work. Mr. Lord, as manager, holds himself personally responsible for the progress of every pupil.

SALEM 1626-1897

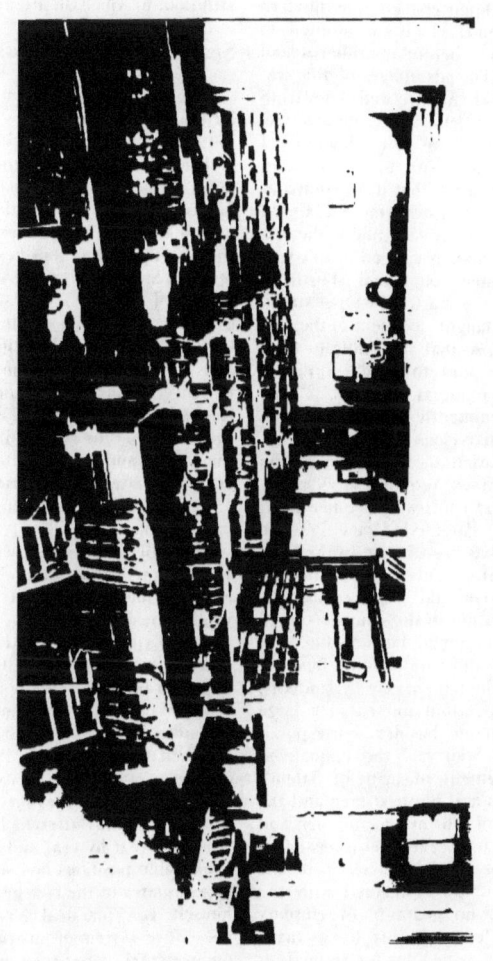

The standing of each is reported to him weekly and a tabulated record of this is kept. Instruction is entirely individual, save in arithmetic and law, for which carefully graded classes are organized. This school is headquarters for the modern Gregg's shorthand, which was adopted in December, 1893, before any other school in America. The advantages of this system are manifold and are well known to the public of Salem and vicinity. Its strongest features are the abolition of shades, angles and positions. This makes the system so natural that it is, comparatively speaking, but a slight mental burden to learn it. So purely scientific is the system that the school has been enabled to originate a system of actual shorthand practice from the start. In typewriting, the student is taught to operate the machine by touch, so that he is able to transcribe his notes and to do his ordinary work without looking at the keys. That this system is eminently practical, all who inspected the marvelous typewritten work which was awarded the first prize at the exhibit of the Essex Agricultural society at Peabody in 1897 can testify. Since May, 1895, Sadler's Patented Office Practice from the Start has been in use in the business department. This is a method of teaching business and bookkeeping by actually duplicating in the school room all the conditions of actual business life. A national bank and various other business concerns, conducted entirely by students, are in active operation and entail a large amount of genuine business correspondence. The school has the unqualified written endorsement of many of Salem's leading bankers and business men and the great number of worthy young men and women placed in excellent positions is the strongest proof of the efficiency of the employment bureau connected with the school. While no guaranty of employment is given, every facility for securing information as to openings for trained office help is at the command of Mr. Lord, and his extensive business acquaintance makes it comparatively easy for a young man, who is able to win his commendation, to secure a position. If some idea of the high character of this school has been gained from a perusal of this article, its purpose will have been accomplished and it only remains to assure the reader that every favorable impression will be confirmed by a personal inspection of the institution, to which all are welcome.

Spence & Peaslee Business College.

One of the best known and most popular educational institutions in this city or section is the Spence & Peaslee Business college, which occupies the entire upper floor, measuring 5400 square feet, in the handsomest building in Salem - the Gardner building, at 210 Essex street. Both the shorthand and business departments of the school date from 1891. The proprietor of the school is F. Arthur Spence, a native of Salem, a graduate of the Salem high school and of Brown University and a practical accountant of large experience. From the beginning, Mr. Spence has had charge of the business department. Early in 1893 he acquired an interest in the school and in December of the same year associated with himself Prof. Frank J. Peaslee of New London, N. H. During the summer of 1897, Mr. Spence assumed full proprietorship of the school. In this practical age, the classical branch estate of questionable utility to the average youth of ordinary means. Nothing is so useful to young ladies and gentlemen just entering upon the active duties of life as a thorough business training and a practical acquaintance with commercial methods and office work. It is to supply this demand that the Spence & Peaslee Business college is conducted by its principal and proprietor. That the object of the school is realized is fully attested by the large attendance year by year and the number of responsible positions now successfully held by graduates of the college. Mr. Spence himself is a practical business man and his entire system of instruction is based upon actual experience as to the best methods of office work. The curriculum includes general business methods, shorthand, typewriting, drawing, painting and modern languages. In the business department the student is given actual office practice from the start. Each pupil not

only has charge of a set of books, but conducts a regular business correspondence and receives replies by mail, including letters with enclosures of checks, notes, invoices, etc. In short, the student learns business by actually doing business. Every transaction is made clear as regards shipping, making and discounting notes, drawing checks, etc. J. C. Alden, after examining the system used by this college, says: "Twenty-five years' business experience in the office of Messrs. John P. Squire & Co., Boston, warrants me in saying that your business practice system is as near actual business as can be. It is the best I have seen in use." Business law is also critically taught. The Beale System of Simplified Shorthand is used. This system has a successful history of fifteen years in Boston, and its many advantages over other systems are obvious. It has dropped the vowel position; its principles are few in number and without exceptions; it is the briefest system in expression and every character is without doubt as to its absolute meaning. Instruction is individual and the road is opened to each pupil to travel as rapidly as his proficiency will allow. Speed in the use of the typewriter is imparted by the latest methods, including the striking of the keys without looking at them. Mimeograph copying is made an important feature. Contracts, specifications, price lists and legal hearings are practically demonstrated on the typewriter. Modern development of advertising has given a new value to the arts of drawing, designing and painting. A department is now devoted to these branches, in charge of Allen L. Herrick, an experienced engraver and water color painter. Tuition will be moderate and the opportunities for training in these arts exceptionally good. A limited number of pupils will

F. ARTHUR SPENCE.

also be taken to private classes in reading, speaking in the Spanish and French languages. A pamphlet containing all the

mation will be mailed upon application. Special effort is made by the management of the college to assist graduates to positions. Among business men of Boston, Spence & Peaslee graduates have acquired the reputation of satisfying the most exacting conditions. The list of public men to whom the college refers by permission and the high character of the testimonials in its catalogue would seem to be sufficient to convince any of the sterling quality of the work of this most practical institution

tractive, the snow white walls and creamy woodwork reflecting the sunshine into every corner, but also being off the street, they are always perfectly quiet. The two class rooms, moreover, are separated by folding doors, so that at any time they can be thrown into one. Although this school has been but two years in Salem, it was founded in Beverly ten years ago. So many of its pupils have, during all the years of its existence, come from the surrounding towns, that Mr. Walker, at the

BANK AT SPENCE & PEASLEE BUSINESS COLLEGE

Mr. Walker's School.

the school is by no means confined to preparation for college. It embraces besides, all the studies of a higher grade grammar school and a first-class high school. The two great advantages of the school are the complete freedom which it offers in the choice of studies, and the individual training in classes. All of the classes are so small that every member gets almost constant attention. Some classes, in fact, have only one member. More than this, if a pupil, for any reason, can do better by himself than in a class with others, he works and recites alone. Sometimes there have been, at the same time, two separate classes using the same textbook, but one somewhat farther advanced than the other. In Mr. Walker's school, which is the only one of its kind this side of Boston, we have thus a revival of the old New England academy system which left so strong an impress of its thorough work upon the minds and characters of our grandfathers.

Frank M. Collester.

In August, 1896, the school committee of the city of Salem made a heavy requisition upon the Murdock school of Winchendon in their unanimous choice of Frank M. Collester as principal of the high school, to succeed A. L. Goodrich. Mr. Collester takes the highest rank as an educator and brought to this city ripe scholarship coupled with years of practical experience as an instructor. He is a native of Gardner, the son of Thornley Collester, one of the pioneers in the chair industry of that town, and is now forty-two years of age. The family is an old and influential one, dating back to the settlement of the town. Principal Collester graduated from Amherst college with the class of '77 and in the fall of the same year took charge of the high school of his own town, remaining nine years. In 1886 he accepted the Winchendon position and while awaiting the completion of the new Murdock building assumed charge of the high school. From his earliest school days, Mr. Collester has been marked in his quickness of perception and his aptitude for study. He was interested in athletics but never to the neglect of the more serious matters of school work. He was most punctual even in the minor affairs and possessed of many other traits which gave an earnest of the success which he has so abundantly achieved. Mr. Collester was gifted in a mechanical way and also talented in vocal music. He sang with the college glee club and filled ap-

FRANK M. COLLESTER.
Principal of Salem High School.

pointments in the town churches. During his comparatively short residence in Salem, Mr. Collester has fulfilled every expectation and the administration of high school affairs has been of the best. He is an active Mason, a past master of the blue lodge, past high priest of the chapter and a Knight Templar. His Masonic membership has been transferred to this city.

Harmony Grove Cemetery.

Over sixty years ago, in February, 1837 a meeting was held and the first steps taken towards the establishment of a rural cemetery in Salem. The financial panic of that year delayed action somewhat, but in 1839 a sufficient amount of money had been subscribed to allow of the purchase of thirty-five acres of land, known as Harmony Grove. The general work was pushed forward rapidly and Feb 19, 1840, the enterprise was incorporated, guaranteeing permanency and freedom from encroachment. The formal consecration occurred June 14 of the same year. During the six decades of the cemetery's history, many improvements have been made in accordance with the customs and ideas of the times, but ever with the single thought of preserving and adding to the natural beauties of the spot, which are unusually striking. Of recent years, endowments providing for the perpetual care of lots have increased in number rapidly. The cemetery is now in the care of a board of nine trustees, with Arthur L. Huntington as president. The superintendent, George W. Creesy, has his office upon the grounds. He is a life long resident of Salem, and with the exception of a period when he learned the carpenter's trade, has been connected with the cemetery affairs since his school days, first as an assistant to his father and since 1880 as superintendent and general manager. Mr. Creesy is a thoroughly practical gardener and florist and has charge of the extensive greenhouses connected with the cemetery. Mr. Creesy was one of the organizers and is deeply interested in the affairs of the Association of American Cemetery Superintendents and is now serving his second year as president of the same. His management of the cemetery has always been such as to command the confidence of all desirous of honoring the departed by a beautiful resting place, such as is found in Harmony Grove.

GEORGE W. CREESY.
Harmony Grove.

Willard J. Hale.

Register of Deeds Willard J. Hale was appointed to his present responsible position, Aug. 31, 1897, to succeed the late Charles S. Osgood. In the fall of the same year he was the nominee of both the leading parties for the office and was elected by a practically unanimous vote. This is by no means Mr. Hale's first experience in places of trust. In his native city of Newburyport, where he obtained his education, he was chosen to the common council in 1879, serving two years, and in 1881 was made chairman, being twice re-elected. As a republican, he represented his district with great credit in the lower branch of the legislature of 1885, and in the following year went to Colorado Springs to engage in real estate transactions. Mr. Hale divided his time between his western interests and the dry goods business at Newburyport, in which he has been interested for himself since twenty years of age. He was appointed postmaster by President Harrison, Sept. 19, 1890, and held the office for four years. In 1896, he was one of the delegates to the republican national convention from the sixth congressional district, and was a member of the committee which officially notified Vice President Hobart of his nomination. Mr. Hale is president of the Board of Trade, a director of the First National Bank, also a trustee of the Five Cents Savings Bank, all of Newburyport. Since an early age, Mr. Hale has been connected with his native city's best interests, and the esteem in which he is held by his townsmen and the people of the entire county is sufficiently told in the high honors which have been conferred upon him.

Late Thomas A. Devine.

In the midst of the active duties of life, Thomas A. Devine was stricken to his death on the evening of Wednesday, May 19, 1897. The report of his demise, so entirely unexpected, was a great shock to the citizens of Salem and it was hardly believed at the first that he who had been so long and favorably known in business and social life had passed away. Mr. Devine was a native of this city and was born Sept. 25, 1850. He was educated in the public schools, leaving at an early age to begin work as back boy in the spinning department of the Naumkeag mills. After learning the trade of a barber, he entered the service of his brother, the late Patrick H.

WILLARD J. HALE, REGISTER OF DEEDS.

Devine, as a driver in the liquor business, and until the time of his death was largely interested in this trade. Of late, Mr. Devine had been considered the largest dealer in this section of the state outside of Boston, having a large wholesale and retail establishment on Merrimac street in Boston, in addition to his business in Salem. He was greatly interested in the

LATE THOMAS A. DEVINE.

East Chattanooga Land Co., being a heavy stockholder and director, also a director of the First National Bank. Shortly before his death he was elected president of the Puritan Brewing Co. His interest in public affairs was most earnest. He had been for years a member of the democratic city and state committees and for three successive times was chosen as a delegate to the national convention of the party. Mr. Devine was a welcome guest at all social functions, among his connections being with the Massachusetts Democratic Club, Div. 5, A. O. H., Veragua council, K. of C., Boston lodge of Elks, and Knights of St. Rose. He attended the Immaculate Conception church and gave most abundantly to charitable and benevolent enterprises, but without ostentation or publicity. He had traveled extensively, crossing the ocean several times and meeting many notables. By his genial and abundant wit, companionable humor and business integrity, Mr. Devine had gained the esteem and respect of all, even of those who had a disagreement with him upon many questions of policy. There survive, a widow and three sons.

Edward A. Mackintire.

Edward Augustus Mackintire is a native of Rhode Island, born in Providence, Jan. 24, 1851, son of John and Clarissa (Craig) Mackintire. His father was of a family of seafaring men in Salem, with the exception of Samuel Mackintire, who was a noted carver and architect during the first decade of the present century. His parents were of Scotch descent. He received a good grammar school education, and at thirteen years of age was at work in the book and stationery store of Henry P. Ives in Salem. Here he learned the business, and remained until 1878, when in February, he formed a partnership with W. Harvey Merrill, under the firm name of Merrill & Mackintire, and opened a book, stationery and wall paper store of his own. In July, 1894, he purchased his partner's interest and continued the business as sole proprietor. Mr. Mackintire has always taken a deep interest in the welfare and growth of Salem, and has by his influence promoted many important improvements. He has been for some years an active member of the Salem Board of Trade, and its president during 1893 and 1894. He was a leading spirit in the establishment of the Salem Co-operative Bank and is now its president; he was for two years a director of the Association of Massachusetts Co-operative Banks. He was also long connected with the Salem Mutual Benefit association and a director of the organization for fifteen years. He is a member of the Essex Institute, of the Salem Charitable Mechanic association, of the Salem Veteran Cadets, of the Enterprise Fire club, and of numerous fraternal organizations; connected with Essex lodge and Naumkeag encampment of Odd Fellows, the Royal Arcanum, the Knights of Honor, the Pilgrim Fathers, Order Scottish Clans, and the United Workmen. In politics he is a republican, interested in the party organization, but never holding office, although many times urged to take nominations. He was an early member of the Salem Republican Flambeau club, and its treasurer for nine years. He was married March 9, 1880, to Miss Alice Williams Glover, a descendant of Gen. John Glover of Marblehead, the famous hero of the Revolution. They have had four children, Bessie Glover, Richard Craig, Alice and George Augustus (deceased).

Salem Hat and Bonnet Bleachery.

This establishment, located at 268 Essex street, is one of the oldest of its kind in the state and so well known to all old Salem residents as to constitute a landmark. The business was inaugurated thirty-five years ago by William A. Clapp, and was operated by him until July, 1896, when it was purchased by the present proprietor, M. D. Webber, Jr., who has fully maintained the reputation for reliability, so long established. Ladies' straw hats and bonnets and men's straw hats are here cleansed, colored and pressed into any desired shape. Feathers are also cleaned, colored and curled. The most modern appliances are employed, and only work of the highest character is done, although charges are always reasonable. At least twice a year the bleachery receives new sets of blocks for pressing over hats in conformity with the very latest Parisian styles. A reputation has been built up, which extends not only to the suburbs but outside the state, as the list of regular customers includes people in all parts of New England. The ladies of Essex county, especially, appreciate this old and reliable establishment, and by patronizing it they have saved many a millinery bill.

B. S. S. Milton.

B. S. S. Milton, with store at 15 St. Peter street, does a large business in the manufacture and sale of proprietary medicines, essences, extracts, sticky and poison fly paper, etc. He is the owner of Milton's Syrup of White Pine Compound, and controls the sale of Russell's Sarsaparilla and Red Clover and of Joy's inks, supplying the latter commodity in large quantities to schools throughout the county. Mr. Milton visits every city and town in Essex county and several in Middlesex county, selling entirely to dealers. At his Salem store, a line of stationery, blank books, order books, confectionery, cigars, etc., is carried. Mr. Milton was born in Rowley in 1841 and came to Salem when seventeen years of age. At first he was employed in the grocery business, but for over thirty years has been in his present line of work. He is a war veteran, enlisting in Co. H, First Massachusetts Cavalry, and was discharged for disability by reason of severe injuries and wounds. Mr. Milton is a member of Phil Sheridan post, G. A. R., House of Sol, and Jerusalem senate, K. A. L. O. of Salem, John Sumner council, O. U. A. M. of Newburyport, and Lynn commandery, Knights of Malta.

EDWARD A. MACKINTIRE.

SALEM 1626-1897

The Upton Paine Studio.

The stranger visiting the historic spots of Salem may not be wholly unfamiliar with the quaint souvenir china displayed in the window of "Hepzibah's Shop," in "The House of the Seven Gables," and may also be interested to learn something of the origin and development of this, without doubt, the first typical souvenir in the world. The witch as painted to-day is the result of fourteen years of study and effort to please patrons of every taste, and in making a selection, one can choose the expression of any emotion a souvenir witch is capable of feeling. Originally, the souvenir was painted in oil colors on pebbles, and the witch figure was selected as typical of Salem. The pebble was discarded, and china selected and is now used altogether. The painter of the witches is a dweller in "The House of the Seven Gables," and, as I. F. Upton, is known all over the world. The Gift Shop connected with the Upton-Paine studios not only contains an endless variety of souvenirs, but a large assortment of richly decorated china, which all are cordially invited to inspect at the Upton-Paine studios, 252 Essex street.

J. Henry Upton.

One of the most talented musicians in Salem is J. Henry Upton. Mr. Upton studied for several years at the Boston Conservatory of Music, New England Conservatory of Music and with Joshua Phippen a magnificent preparation for his duties in connection with the instruction of pupils upon the piano forte and the organ. Mr. Upton is a versatile artist, appearing at functions where music from dancing numbers to the highest classical compositions are in order. He is rapidly acquiring a reputation as a composer, the favorite of his works being The Serysa Two Step. Mr. Upton has played upon the organ at a number of churches, now acting in this capacity at the Universalist churches in Salem and Marblehead. To these accomplishments, he adds a thorough knowledge of the practical workings of the piano forte, thus being enabled to do tuning.

Henrietta F. Upton.

Hensetta F. Upton, instructor in oratory and physical culture, with rooms at 252 Essex street, spent three years at the Emerson College of Oratory, studying for her chosen vocation. Miss Upton is most favorably known in Salem, having spent her entire life here, and coming of a gift of finish. In the way of elocution, the great object sought after is individuality, correct expression being the logical se

HENRIETTA F. UPTON.   **J. HENRY UPTON.**

quence. The science of visible speech is fully considered, as is that of gesture. Along with general physical culture, the voice is also given a course of training. Classes are formed in or out of Salem, for which special rates are given.

Henry O. Upton.

Mr. Upton was born in North Salem in 1839, and with the exception of eight years spent in Boston, has continued a resident of this city. After returning to Salem, he attended the Browne school, and at sixteen years of age learned the tinsmith's trade. At this time Mr. Upton became a member of the First Universalist church choir and sang there for a number of years. Being possessed of a good tenor voice, his services were sought elsewhere; and he served as chorister in other churches. Mr. Upton was a member of the Salem Brass band and one of the original members of the Salem Cadet band. He was appointed teacher of music in the public schools in 1883, which position he successfully filled for five years. During this period he composed several songs which were eminently suited to children's voices. As a musical composer he has attained a reputation which is more than local. In 1864, he began the study of society dancing and graceful deportment, and opened his first class in Gothic hall, Danvers. He has taught dancing every season since then, and his many pupils are a proof of his ability and success as a teacher. Mr. Upton is held in high esteem by the professors of dancing, and is a member of the American National Association of Masters of Dancing.

HENRY O. UPTON.

T. T. SAVORY.

T. T. Savory.

One of the older and well-known citizens of Salem is T. T. Savory, who, since 1850 has been engaged in the expressing business, operating between here and Boston. He was born in this city, has always lived and been identified with the best interests of the locality. He served two years in the State legislature, representing his district in 1896-7. He is a thirty-second degree Mason. Having for many years resided and done business in this city Mr. Savory needs no introduction.

SALEM 1626-1897

REV. E. P. FARNHAM

years, w... ... ... of sickness in ... family, ... moved to Monroe, his where he remained six years. Mr. Latham is now in his tenth year of successful ... with the First Baptist church of this city, during ever battling ... to which ... ces. During the past five great progress and ... movement have been made in all departments of the work. With a full a...ecation of the importance ... religious activity ... ng the young, he has entered this ... with ... e vigor, having been a member of the Young People's Society of Christian Endeavor since coming into this state. For several years he served as a vice-president of the society, and upon the board of directors. Although previously declining the presidency, Mr. Farnham yielded to the pressure upon him in ... 1896 and accepted the honor, serving one term and refusing a re-election. He has written largely for religious and secular periodicals. A notable series of articles dealt with the general subject of Protestantism in America. Mr. Farnham has taken a large interest in public affairs

and was president of the Kindergarten association, under whose auspices kindergarten instruction was offered the children of this city until the growing sentiment caused the acceptance of the idea by the public school authorities.

First Baptist Church.

The First Baptist ... w...
... ... The
... ... Rev ... Beat ... D
... ... First of ...
Wednesday, ...
... ...
... the First Baptist church ... D
... ... w ... ...
... ...
... ...
... ...
... ...
... ...
... ...

FIRST BAPTIST CHURCH.

bers, the present number being 338, of whom fifteen have been in membership for more than fifty years. The Sunday school was established in 1818, and now numbers 300. There are also connected with the church a woman's home and foreign missionary society, a society of junior endeavor, a girl's mission band and a Sunday school for the Armenians. The church has always taken a prominent part in the affairs of the denomination, its pastors and members having from time to time been connected with the boards of the several state and missionary societies, since its first pastor was chosen secretary of the Board of Missions, June 2, 1826. His successors as pastors have been: Rev. Rufus Babcock, D. D., installed Aug. 23, 1826; Rev. John Wayland, D. D., installed Aug. 6, 1834; Rev. Thos. D. Anderson, D. D., installed Mar. 15, 1842; Rev. Robt. C. Mills, D. D., June 14, 1848; Rev. Geo. E. Merrill, D. D., installed Feb. 1, 1877; Rev. Galusha Anderson, D. D., installed Oct. 16, 1885; Rev. Edwin P. Farnham, installed June 1, 1888. The present church treasurer is Charles H. Price, elected December, 1856; the clerk is Nathl. A. Very, elected Sept., 1869; the superintendent of the Bible school is Hon. Henry C. Leach, serving except an interval of two years since 1885.

The First Church.

The organization of this, the first church in Salem, by virtue of its dating back to 1634, makes it the oldest protestant society in the United States and in its possession old Salem bears her distinction gracefully. The original edifice shown in a previous page now stands back of the Essex Institute building and is visited by thousands of sight seers yearly. The original site at the corner of Essex and Washington sts. is still maintained, but a handsome and imposing structure now serves the use of the society, showing in marked contrast to the original one story affair now of such historic interest. In 1670 a second edifice was erected on the same land, the former edifice being resumed for the use of the town as a school and watch house and was used for these purposes for nearly a century afterwards. In 1760 the town having secured better quarters for a public building, the old structure was removed to the premises of Thornton Proctor, and used for a tavern and other purposes, for another hundred years. Through the beneficence of Francis Peabody the building was presented to the Essex Institute, and has since been kept as a curiosity,—and a great relic it is indeed.

FIRST CHURCH UNITARIAN.

The present edifice of this society was remodelled about 1874 and comprises one of the handsomest structures used for religious worship. The interior is attractive, and especially within the past few years the church has experienced a marked growth in membership. Many of the leading families of the locality are numbered among its members, and the services are invariably well attended. A feature of the church service is the excellent music rendered. The present pastor of this historic church of the Unitarian denomination is very popular in Salem.

REV. E. J. PRESCOTT
was born in Hampton Falls, N. H., Aug. 27, 1865. His early life was spent on a farm owned by his grandparents, who were of the worthy and substantial New England stock, seven generations of which have lived in the same town in unbroken succession. At the age of twenty, Mr. Prescott entered the preparatory department of the Meadville Theological school, where he remained five years, graduating in 1890. He then added a course of study at Harvard University, and at the Emerson College of Oratory. In the fall of 1890, a call to the First Congregational society of Littleton was accepted, and Mr. Prescott remained two years. He was next located at Kennebunk, Me., for five years, the call to this, the second oldest church in the state, coming to him. He began his work with the pastorate of Chapel Street, April 1, 1897, since which time there has been a marked increase in matters of interest, spiritual, as well as numerical.

tury. The corner stone of the church on Rust street was laid Aug. 17, 1808 and the dedication occurred in June of the following year. The early records of the church have been lost, and so strong was the prejudice against the Universalist movement that the papers of that day made no reference to the doings of this people. The exterior of the church building remained essentially unconstructed until the middle 70s, when it was remodeled quite extensively. The list of pastors follow: Rev. Edward Turner, Hosea Ballou, Joshua Flagg, Barnard Street, Seth Stetson, Leonard W[...], Matthew H. Smith, Lucius S. Everett, John Brodie, Sumner [...] W. [...] Sheath[...], Edwin C. Bolles, Nehemiah Roger, Charles H. Pennoyer. The present incumbent is Rev. [...]

REV. E. J. PRESCOTT

First Universalist Church.

The first services of those of the Universalist faith in Salem were held in the fall of 1804, at the old Court House, followed by others soon after at the house of Nathaniel [...], then by preachers including Rev. John Murray, Thomas Barnes, Thomas Jones, Hosea Ballou, Edward Turner and other leading local clergymen of the earlier part of the present century.

People's Christian Universalist, eighty-five [...] its sixtieth. in their respective [...] Free Church Messenger, a weekly issued in the last of the [...] edited by the pastor. Twelve years ago the church edifice at approximate cost of $20,000 and church work now progressing satisfactorily.

Rev. Clark H. Plumley has served as pastor of the First Universalist church at Salem since July, 1893.

SALEM 1626-1897

FIRST UNIVERSALIST CHURCH.

at which time he received a unanimous call to this field. He was born at Monmouth, Ill., Jan. 8, 1859, and was reared in the town of Stafford, Connecticut. Here he received a common school education, following this by study at Monson academy and Tufts college, graduating from the latter institution with the class of '83. In his preparatory and college days, Mr. Puffer devoted a considerable portion of the time to teaching. Leaving college, he joined the staff of the Springfield Republican, later taught at Arms academy, Shelburne Falls, and for five years was of the faculty of Washburn college, Kansas. In September, 1889, he entered the Tufts Divinity school for a one year's course, being then ordained and installed over the Universalist church at Stoughton, where he remained for three years and three months, when the Salem call was accepted. In Stoughton, Mr. Puffer was honored in positions of responsibility, among others being membership upon the board of education and the presidency of the Old Colony Association. He is now chaplain of the house of correction in this city, for three years has served as chairman of the press committee of the Anti-saloon League, through whose efforts so much has been accomplished for the temperance cause. He is one of the four missionary superintendents having in charge the denominational work in Essex county, and for two years was a member of the visiting committee of Tufts Divinity school. He is affiliated with the Masons and Odd Fellows.

Central Baptist Church.

This church sprang from the First Baptist society and was formed by thirty-two members who were dismissed for the purpose of forming a new church, in 1826. A church edifice was erected on St. Peter street, which has since been noticeably improved, and dedicated June 8, 1826. The first regular pastor was Rev. George Learned, who was ordained August 23, 1826. Compelled by ill health to resign, Mr. Learned was succeed-

REV. CHARLES H. PUFFER.

ed by Rev. Robert E. Pattison, who presided over the young and growing church to 1830. He was followed by Rev. Cyrus P. Grosvenor, who was pastor to 1834, and succeeded by Rev. Joseph Banvard, who acceptably filled the pulpit for nine years. In 1846, Rev. Benjamin Brierly was ordained and continued as pastor for two years. From 1849 to 1854, Rev. Wm. H. Eaton was pastor. He was superseded in 1855 by Rev. Daniel D. Winn, who, in 1867, was followed by Rev. S. Hartwell Pratt. Rev David Weston occupied the pulpit for a few months only, in 1872, and was succeeded by Rev. W. H. H. Marsh, who, after a pastorate of seven years and a half was followed by Rev. Charles A. Towne. Rev. Samuel B. Nobbs was the next pastor, who remained two years and nine months. He was succeeded by Rev. Harry M. Warren, Sept. 1, 1894, who continued until the following February. Since Sept. 1, 1896, the church has had for its pastor Rev R. M. Martin, D. D. The church is centrally located and invariably the services are well attended, there being 332 communicants. The Sunday school is a large and prosperous one, and the superintendent, LeRoy B. Philbrick, has just concluded his twenty fifth year as its superintendent. Although marked improvements have been made to the church edifice in years gone by, those recently wrought have been the most important in the improvement of the structure. Among these improvements are the putting in of a new organ, the complete remodeling of the interior with new floor, pew furnishings and interior decoration.

CENTRAL BAPTIST CHURCH.

The gallery has also been improved and the pulpit remodelled. Although the seating capacity has been necessarily lessened, the church has been sufficiently beautified and improved to warrant the vast expenditure made. The present pastor,

REV. R. M. MARTIN, D. D.,

is a native of Scotland, and immigrated to Lonsdale, R. I., with his parents when he was ten years old. He was graduated at Brown University in 1873. After teaching Latin in Peddie Institute, Hightstown, N. J., one year, he entered Rochester Theological seminary, Rochester, N. Y., from which he graduated in 1877, being a classmate of Rev. F. P. Farnham of the First Baptist church of this city, in both college and seminary. Previous to coming to Salem he held several pastorates, his last being at the Fourth Baptist church of Providence, R. I. He closed his pastorate there to go to Rochester to pursue a desired study in Exegetics and in the New Testament introduction. In connection with his post graduate course he was for one year preacher at the First Baptist church in Buffalo. In Dr. Martin the Central Baptist church have an able preacher and kind and sympathetic pastor.

Prospect Hill.

The distinguishing feature of the real estate business of the last decade is that of the developing and placing upon the market of tracts of land within more or less easy access to cities and the larger towns, putting within the reach of persons of moderate means, homes retired from the over-crowded thoroughfares of industrial centres. In the front rank of the better grades of property managed with this idea in view must be placed the land of the Prospect Hill Syndicate in the city of Beverly. The property covers an area of sixty-seven acres and includes the rough, breezy highland, formerly known as the Bancroft estate. For many years it has been a favorite resort for those desiring the freest air and a magnificent view of the surrounding country. In all Essex county, there is not a more sightly spot. The ocean is discernible from Beverly Harbor to Misery Island, the Willows, Marblehead Neck and Naugus Head being in full view. The buildings in Salem can be easily distinguished, as can the principal points in Peabody and Danvers, including the beautiful asylum grounds, Wenham, Topsfield and Essex. The central location of the property caused it to be considered for some time in connection with public uses, notably for park purposes. The latter was the cherished idea of leading Beverly citizens for years, the late Hon. John I. Baker being particularly interested in the project. The late Lucy Larcom, the eminent poetess, was also acquainted with the vicinity through her long residence in Beverly, and wrote most enthusiastically of the loveliness and charm of the spot. The park project of the earlier day, which was intended to include the entire estate, failed of consummation, and the syndicate owning the property have expended much time and money in planning and building of fine avenues upon the more elevated portions to render it available for residential purposes. The higher sections of the property have been developed into about two hundred beautiful building sites, which they offer for sale. The advantages of Beverly as a place of residence are manifold. Although the youngest of Bay State cities, it is exceedingly rich in promise. Conveniently removed from Boston, the Boston & Maine road gives first-class service in all directions, a branch road reaching to Gloucester and Rockport, meeting the main line at this point. By electrics, the entire country surrounding is within easy reach for trips of business or pleasure, the latter phase of traveling possibilities being no small factor in such a territory as the noted North Shore of Essex county. One electric line passes the hill on Essex street, and the other over Cabot street within three minutes' walk of Prospect Hill, and the Beverly and Montserrat stations on the Boston & Maine are near by. The city has the best postal, telegraph and telephone facilities, gas and electricity for lighting, domestic and manufacturing purposes, and the famous pure water of Wenham lake has already been brought upon the hill, although the elevation is 100 to 125 feet above the sea level. The main approach from the city is by way of Essex street, lately widened through the munificence of the syndicate, to fifty-five feet. The city hall can be reached in a few minutes by this street and a new and costly schoolhouse has been lately erected in the neighborhood. The principal avenues upon the hill are known by such names as Baker, Whitney, Boyden, Giddings, Lefavour, Larcom, Appleton, Clark, Bancroft, Peabody, Sargent and Odell, aggregating in length 10,750 feet, or over two miles. Reasonable restrictions are placed upon all building projects, with the idea of securing harmony for the residences built upon the property. For a single house the minimum is $2,000, with $3,000 for a double dwelling, although upon the northern slope a $1,500 building may be constructed. Houses must be at least ten feet removed from the street, making a width of fifty feet practically seventy feet. Over fifty lots have already been sold, upon a number of which fine residences have been erected, but magnificent sites, each from 4,500 to 8,000 square feet in size, still remain and afford an exceptional opportunity to those desiring a home in a select locality. Henry W. Peabody, A. D. S. Bell and Frank E. Locke are the trustees of the syndicate, and any desired information will be cheerfully furnished by the authorized agents, viz.: Frank E. Locke, 81 Washington street, Salem; Charles F. Lee, Beverly; and J. L. Nason & Co., 21 School street, Boston.

SALEM 1626-1897

VIEW ON PROSPECT HILL, SHOWING SALEM WILLOWS TO THE RIGHT.

Montserrat.

Just beyond Prospect Hill in Beverly is the land of the Montserrat Syndicate, of which Henry W. Peabody, Leland H. Cole and Frank E. Locke are trustees. The location is among the most beautiful of the many charming spots between Beverly and Cape Ann. The Montserrat station, the prettiest upon the Gloucester branch, is situated in the midst of level fields of the richest green and in the background are forests of apparently boundless extent. The distance to Boston is nineteen miles, eleven trains each way daily, at suitable hours, furnishing the best communication with the Hub. The favorite train of Montserrat dwellers having business in Boston, is the express leaving the former place at 8.18 A. M., making the run in thirty minutes without stop. At 4.30 in the afternoon, also, one may leave Boston on a train running without stop to Montserrat, alighting as the clocks are marking the hour of five. Other trains stop at Beverly, Salem and Lynn, making this a most desirable place of residence for those having business in any of these cities. Electric cars to and from Gloucester pass half-hourly, reaching to Rockport, the extreme point of land on the east, and connecting at Beverly for Salem, Lynn, Peabody, Danvers and many other cities and towns in Essex and Middlesex counties. The Beverly city hall is but one mile distant. North of the steam railroad station is Montserrat avenue and still adjacent, the park of the same name. This park has been laid with much care and expense, after plans by F. L. & J. C. Olmsted, the noted designers of this class of improvements. Beyond the Park about 200 feet north of the depot is Colon street, upon which is the extensive frontage of Montserrat Highlands, richly wooded with pines and all varieties of hard wood, wild shrubs, ferns, etc., as picturesque as the hills of New Hampshire. The total area of the elevation is about ninety acres, bounded easterly by Brimble avenue, eighty feet wide, and westerly by Heather lane. From several points, magnificent sea views are to be obtained of the bay, the islands and the shore of Marblehead. Lookout Rock, directly opposite the depot, is a particularly sightly spot, and a favorite resort for parties in quest of scenic effects. Such is the character of the scenery surrounding this extensive and attractive section that artists with brush and pencil are not infrequently seen sketching favorable spots within the bounds of the land. A winding way has been built to Lookout Rock from Colon street, opposite Spring street, as an avenue might be built with any grade. This may be used afoot or as a bridle-path. Carriages have access by a drive from Colon street, near Heather lane, and it is possible to drive around the rocks, in full sight of the charming water view. An important advantage of this locality is that it is cool in summer by reason of the southerly breezes from the sea over a mile away and the east winds are pleasantly tempered by the miles of forest that they traverse. In winter the wooded highlands protect from the fierce northerly blasts. To the south are many fine summer places, roads leading through cool and shady woodland. The Central square of Montserrat Park as arranged by the Messrs. Olmsted, is to be always open, and within the other two squares are nineteen lots of about 8000 square feet each, most desirable for those who have business in Boston, Salem, Lynn or Beverly; many other lots are being developed upon Essex, Colon, Corning and Pearl streets, &c. An important restriction in the construction of houses upon the syndicate property is that each must be of a minimum cost of $2,500. The attention of any who contemplate the establishment of a country or seaside home is invited to this property, which comprises the advantages of both, and will be sold at moderate price for such occupancy. With so many conveniences, a summer residence at this point could be made desirable for a permanent home. Frank E. Locke, 81 Washington street, Salem, will be pleased to furnish printed matter or any other information to those who may be interested in securing a home in this most desirable locality. Application may also be made to Charles F. Lee, Beverly, or J. L. Nason & Co., School street, Boston.

OCEAN VIEW, MONTSERRAT.

Frank E. Locke.

Through his connection with the Prospect Hill and Montserrat syndicates, Frank E. Locke has become one of the best known of the real estate men of this vicinity. He acts as one of the trustees and as treasurer of both projects, representing a capital of $85,000. Mr. Locke makes a specialty of taking charge of estates, a large number of which have been entrusted to his care. He takes a personal interest in all business committed to him, ensuring perfect satisfaction to all concerned. He is considered to be an expert in regard to valuation of property in and about Salem. Mr. Locke is a native of this city and was born June 16, 1860. He attended the public schools, after which he entered the employment of Charles G. Fogg, the firm formerly being known as Guy Bros., and dealing in crockery. Mr. Locke rose to the position of head salesman, later accepting a clerical position with the Salem Marine Insurance company, also acting as clerk for William Northey. Here Mr. Locke began the work of which he now makes a specialty, remaining with the Marine company for twelve years, until it closed up its affairs and went out of business. He still conducts a fire, marine and life insurance agency in connection with his real estate engagements, representing strong companies. He is also qualified as a justice of the peace and notary public. Mr. Locke takes a lively interest in public affairs and is a member of the Essex Institute and a director and treasurer of the Salem Fraternity. He is also treasurer of Puritan lodge, A. O. U. W. and Asiatic lodge, N. E. O. P.

FRANK E. LOCKE.

William D. Dennis.

A man held in high esteem by his fellow citizens, shown to some degree in the positions of trust and other matters of public import committed to his care, is William Devereux Dennis. He is a native of Salem, born October 11, 1847, and has always made his home in this city. His profession, that of architecture, came largely as a natural gift, his father, Devereux Dennis, having been a prominent carpenter and builder in an earlier day. Mr. Dennis is easily the leader in his line in the city and besides an immense volume of work for private parties, has designed the greater part of the construction and remodeling of public buildings in Salem of recent years. For a long period he has had charge of the mechanical department of the evening drawing school. He is a prominent Odd Fellow, being a past grand of Essex lodge, a past grand patriarch of Naumkeag encampment, and a past district deputy; he is also connected, as an officer, with other organizations, including the Royal Arcanum and the Naumkeag Fire club. He is active in the First Universalist church and serves as chairman of the standing committee. He is also president of the Massachusetts Universalist State Convention, to which position he was chosen at its last annual session. He was a chairman of the Republican city committee for three years and represented the fifteenth Essex district with signal success in the lower house of the legislatures of '02, '93, '04. Deserving well of the citizens of Salem, Mr. Dennis may reasonably be not wholly unprepared for calls to higher honors with which his legions of friends insist upon connecting his name.

Hon. Francis Norwood.

Francis Norwood, Beverly, member of the governor's council from the fifth district, was born in Rockport, Mass., January 10, 1841. He is in the seventh generation from Judge Norwood, who gained prominence as one of the regicides of Charles 1st of England. His son, Francis, immigrated to Salem about 1660. From him the successive generations are Joshua (3), Caleb (4), Francis (5), 6 Seth, who was the father of the future councilor. He was a resident in Rockport, and later became the first American manufacturer of isinglass at Ipswich. From this town he moved to Beverly and began the manufacture of boots and shoes in 1858, a business he carried on successfully until his death in 1875. He married Louisa, daughter of William Odell of Topsfield. Francis Norwood came with his father's family to Beverly in 1846, and has since made that place his residence. After receiving all the education offered by the public schools of the town, he went to work with his father at the age of eighteen in the cutting department of the factory. By gradual steps he learned the entire business, and in 1860 he commenced to sell goods as a travelling salesman. In 1865 he became a joint partner, and was manager of the business up to the time of his father's decease. The business was carried on under the title of Seth Norwood & Co., until 1891, when the Seth Norwood Shoe Co. was incorporated with Francis Norwood as president. From early in his life Mr. Norwood has been thoroughly identified with the political affairs of Beverly. No small share of his time has been given to services on the town and city committees. His first vote was cast for President Lincoln and from that day to the present he has always voted the straight republican ticket, without the alteration of a single name. Two years were given to services as a member of the state central committee, and he was a past experience made him a valued member. He was elected to the state senate in 1881 and again in 1882, following Col. Jonas H. French in this position. Offered the nomination for a third term he declined in order to give the opportunity to a candidate from a neighboring city. He was, however, succeeded by a democratic senator, and the fact of his being able to wrest a district from his opponents has always been greatly to his credit in republican circles. While in the senate he served on the committees on roads and bridges, manufactures, fisheries, and fed-

WILLIAM D. DENNIS.

eral relations, being chairman of the two last named. He was a member of the electoral college in 1888, and voted for President Harrison. In the campaign of 1896 Mr. Norwood's name was brought forward as a candidate for governor's council from the fifth councillor district.

tutions, prisons, and accounts. As a change seemed necessary in the postmastership of his adopted city, Mr. Norwood was duly nominated for the position and received his commission as postmaster, June 29, 1897. The Beverly Citizen had the following kindly words to say regard-

HON. FRANCIS NORWOOD.

was elected to the state senate, and was re-elected the following year, and made a brilliant showing. Last fall he was nominated for councillor and received an overwhelming majority, running far ahead of his ticket. The "Citizen" joins in extending congratulations to Mr. Norwood, and may his efforts be crowned by success."

He is now serving as one of the trustees of the Beverly Savings bank, succeeding his father in that position in 1875. He is also interested in the Independent Order of Odd Fellows, and is a member of Bass River Lodge. Though often solicitated, Mr. Norwood has persistently declined to accept nominations for town or city offices, though it is safe to say that he could have been elected to various positions. He was a member of the anti-division committee and rendered valuable service in opposing the division of his adopted town. His loyalty to the republican party has been indicated by the faithfulness with which he has voted the straight party ticket; but besides this Mr. Norwood has been a generous promoter of the republican cause for many years to the full extent of his means, and has been active and zealous in political clubs and committees. Through his term of years he has acquired a leading position among the councils of his party, and is recognized among the leaders in his section of the state. Mr. Norwood was married June 12, 1872, to Helen F., daughter of Edward F. Whittredge.

Henry C. Leach.

The chairman of the Salem school board is a representative son of Essex county. Mr. Leach was born in the town of Manchester, Oct. 9, 1832, son of Benjamin Leach and Lucy Story Allen. On his father's side he is descended from Lawrence Leach, a member of Governor Endicott's party which landed in Salem in 1628. Lawrence Leach was one of the first selectmen of the town, and in 1636 was given a grant of one hundred acres of land. He was spoken of by the governor of the company as "a careful and painful man." His son, Robert Leach, removed to Manchester in 1636. A portion of the tract of land

HENRY C. LEACH.

originally granted him is now in the possession of Henry C. Leach, who makes his summer home at this point. The title to the land has remained in the family since 1640. Lucy Story Allen was a descendant of William Allen, who is said to have come to New England from Manchester in the mother country. He was a member of the Dorchester company which settled at Cape Ann in 1624, removing three years later to the settlement at Naumkeag, where Governor Endicott found them upon his arrival in 1628. In 1640, William Allen was one of the petitioners to the general court asking that Jeffries creek might be erected into a village, and he became one of the selectmen of the town of Manchester on its incorporation in 1645. The records of Salem declare him to have been "an influential and enterprising citizen." The subject of this sketch received his early training in the Manchester public schools, graduating from the high school in 1848. For five years he was an apprentice in the furniture business with James H. Beal & Bro. of Boston. Following this he spent three years in study at the Suffield, Conn.

New England Felt Roofing works of Boston. He is prominent in the affairs of the First Baptist church.

Newcomb & Gauss.

In these days of progress nothing is more essential to the success of the business community than up-to-date printing. Salem has been famous for its printers ever since the early days of the colonial period and they have always excelled in the quality of their work. Never have they been so near the front as at the present day and the most convincing proof of the ability of Salem printers to turn out artistic and meritorious work is found within the covers of this book,

NEW WHITLOCK PONY PRESS OF NEWCOMB & GAUSS.

Literary institution. He was engaged in business at St. Louis from 1855, until after the breaking out of the war of the rebellion, spending the summers of 1855-6-7 in Kansas, the troubled days of that exciting period then being at their height. In 1863 he removed to Denver, where he was connected with the house of Tappan & Co., and was active in the political movements which so largely make up the life and interests of a new state. He was for two years a member of the territorial council (senate) and served as president. Returning to New England in 1869, Mr. Leach has since made his home in Salem. For three years he was interested in the hardware trade, but for the past twenty-five years has been connected with the

which was printed by Messrs. Newcomb & Gauss, at the office of the Salem Observer, the only remaining one of our time-honored newspapers. Messrs. Newcomb & Gauss are the successors of Pease, Traill & Fielden, who in turn succeeded to the business of the old-time firm of W. & S. B. Ives, whose imprint is still to be seen on the title page of many a publication of earlier days. The firm is now located in a commodious and well-equipped building next to the City Hall and has the finest plant for the general run of job printing of any office east of Boston, and the quality of work which they turn out on their improved presses is equal to that of any metropolitan office of the highest grade. Within a year two new two-revolution Whitlock presses, especially designed for half-tone cut printing have been added to the already fine equipment in the pressroom, and in type the firm have acquired all the modern faces, so that all the work issuing from their hands has that superior appearance which can only be produced by the possession of the latest and improved type and presses, and the special skill necessary to achieve the best result is not lacking. executed. Special prominence just at this time is given to the proper printing of half-tone cuts and the successful treatment that is accorded them is apparent to all who glance over the pages of this work. Such printing is painstaking in the extreme and requires expert workmen. In printing of directories the office has more than a local reputation, having turned out such requisites for many cities and towns, the best known being

PRESS ROOM NEWCOMB & GAUSS

That Messrs. Newcomb & Gauss have achieved [...] the [...] of [...] [...] so [...] at the [...] that large shares of the business has [...] their rooms and not to any old time concern accustomed to the superior workmanship of the larger offices in the state, and they have to [...] that enable them to maintain the highest standard called [...]. It would be hardly possible to specify the kinds of printing the Newcomb, Boston, Boston [...] [...] [...] [...] the cottages to be with Newcomb & Gauss, and they are [...] from the presses goes all [...] the country. Amongst [...] the [...] a great variety of superior work books and pamphlets of every description, catalogs, town and city reports. In fact the varied lines so successfully cared for by that the growing business demonstrates it is conducted with energy and enterprise.

GOODHUE STREET WORKS, M. ROBSON LEATHER CO.

M. Robson Leather Company.

Salem's second largest industry is also one of the leaders in the United States in the manufacture of its special line of goods. The business of the M. Robson Leather Co., to which is referred, and which is now a close corporation, was founded by Matthew Robson in 1865. After many years of successful business, his interests, with those of Poor Brothers and E. A. Maloon, were consolidated in 1894, forming the present concern which operates two large plants in this city and another at Manistee, Michigan. At the factories of the company, the maximum number of hands employed is between five and six hundred. The product is sent all over the world and comprises finished wax, kip, satin calf, Robson calf, imitation kangaroo and splits of hemlock and combination tannages. The currying is done at the Goodhue street plant, which consists of a large number of buildings covering several acres. At this location is also a large combination tannery where on the average, 8,000 sides of leather are tanned weekly. At Atlantic, a distance of two miles from the Goodhue street works, is a tannery with a capacity of 1,500 sides daily. This large tannery is located apart from the residential section of the city and after being destroyed by fire, was rebuilt and arranged with the view to perfect drainage. At the Manistee plant, the firm has facilities to turn out about 1,000 sides daily. The company is alive to new ideas and inventions and expert millwrights are in constant employ investigating and studying for the most approved machinery. All interested in the enterprise are practical men who have a grasp of every detail of the business, acquired by long and hard experience. The absorbing aim of the managers has always been to produce only goods of superior quality, relying upon merit to obtain business. The magnificent worth of the idea is too obvious to require comment. The city of Salem and the entire vicinity is proud of the great triumph of commercial integrity as typified in the Robson Leather company. A

ATLANTIC TANNERY, M. ROBSON LEATHER CO.

large number of the employees of the concern have been associated with Mr. Robson for many years, among them being Charles Sadler, who for over thirty years has had charge of the currying shop at the Goodhue street works. Largely it is as follows: President, A. F. Poor; treasurer, Matthew Robson; directors, A. F. Poor, J. H. Poor, Matthew Robson, E. A. Mahson and A. H. Bigelow. J. H. Poor and E. A. M......, respectively, of the tannery, and hold department at Balcomb, Brown & Fiske of Boston are the selling agents.

Matthew Robson.

The great M. Robson Leather company derives its name from the treasurer, Matthew Robson. M. Robson came to Salem in 1856, ever since that time has been interested in the leather industry. From humble beginnings, he has risen to his present position as the financier of one of the largest concerns of the kind in the country. In 1895 M. Robson started a currying business which grew rapidly, and in 1897 he consolidated his interests with those of Poor Brothers and E. A. Mahson, resulting in the immense enterprise of to-day. Besides M. Robson associated with him are a

young men with whom he had had greater or less business relations extending over a period of several years. Leaving Indian Orchard of the company to another place, it may be said of Mr. Robson that he is identified with the most substantial and wholesome interests of the city of Salem. He is active in religious work, being a member of the Wesley M. E. church, chairman of the board of trustees of the society and superintendent of the Sunday school. He is greatly interested in the work among young men, and is a member and president of the Salem Y. M. C. A. and chairman of the building committee. He has served in both branches of the legislative department of the city government and is now member of the school board and a trustee of the Salem hospital. M. Robson is also trustee of the Plummer Farm school, a director in the Mercantile National bank, and a member of the investment committee of the Five Cents Savings bank. As a business partner the commercial life of the community for the last sixty-five or firms which at one time and another have done business in Salem. By native ability, honesty and character, Mr. Robson has attained to his present em-

MATTHEW ROBSON, Treasurer M. Robson Leather Co.

nent position and in the prime of manhood enjoys the respect and esteem of all, with everything which goes to make life pleasant. His career is a story of successes and good deeds and furnishes an inspiring lesson to the thoughtful young man of the day.

Albert F. Poor.

In the person of President Albert F. Poor, the M. Robson Leather company has at its head a particularly suitable man, both as a business manager and as a practical tanner. Mr. Poor is of a family of tanners, his father, the late Joseph Poor, having done business in Peabody for over sixty years. A brother, Joseph H., is also connected with the Robson company at the present time as manager of the tannery department in this city and western representative. Albert F. Poor was born in South Danvers, now Peabody, in 1846, and has resided in that town during his entire life. He received a good common school education and at the age of fourteen entered a tannery built and stocked by his father, but managed by his brother, Warren A. Poor. The subject of this sketch served the necessary time in learning every detail of the trade, and in 1870 began manufacturing upon his own account. For several years he was associated with his brother Warren, later doing business alone for twelve years. In 1880, assisted by his brother Joseph, he founded the Atlantic tannery, the same being conducted under the firm name of Poor Brothers until 1893, when the plant was destroyed by fire. The following year, the factory was rebuilt, and consolidation occurred with Matthew Robson, with whom close relations had been maintained for some time. Poor Brothers having done the tanning and Mr. Robson the currying for both concerns. Mr. Poor became president of the allied interests, and is a director and one of the five owners of the close corporation. He is known as a just employer, possessed of the greatest public spirit, and ever thoughtful as to the welfare of the community. His residence at Peabody is one of the most comely and attractive of the many for which that town is noted. He is a director of the Warren National bank of Peabody, a member of the Exchange News room and an Odd Fellow. Mr. Poor is known as one of the influential men of the locality in which he resides.

ALBERT F POOR, PRESIDENT M. ROBSON LEATHER CO.

Joseph H. Poor.

The name of Poor is inseparably associated with the leather industry in the city of Salem at the present time. Joseph H. Poor, the manager of the tannery department in the great Robson concern, is a thoroughly practical leather man, having spent several years at the trade. He was born in Peabody in 1848, the son of the late Joseph Poor, and brother to A. F. Poor, president of the Robson company. The subject of this sketch was educated at the Bowditch school, at the close of his school days engaging in the work in which he has made so eminent a success. His first business venture was in 1877, when he began manufacturing at Salem, later removing to Peabody and continuing there until 1886. He then associated with his brother, A. F. Poor, and the Atlantic tannery was started. In 1894, the Poor interests were consolidated with those of Matthew Robson, although for some time previously the two firms had maintained friendly and intimate business relations. Besides his duties in connection with the tanning department in this city, Mr. Poor is manager of the plant at Manistee, Michigan, and western representative of the concern. He is also treasurer and general manager of the Minnsing Leather Co. of Minnsing, Michigan, whose plant is said to be the sixth largest sole leather establishment in the country. Minnsing is located on Lake Michigan, has a magnificent harbor and every element which would tend to build up a progressive western community. By his great business interests both east and west, Mr. Poor has formed an immense circle of acquaintances scattered over a wide territory, and he has imbibed largely of the enterprising vigor so marked in the newer parts of the country. As one of the five owners in the Robson company, he holds a seat in the board of directors. He is also a director in the National Exchange bank of Salem, director and large owner in the Bay State Belting company, which has a tannery in Salem, factory in South Boston, and office and store on Franklin street, Boston. Mr. Poor is a member of the board of trade. Few manufacturers are possessed of more energy and few indeed better known than J. H. Poor.

RESIDENCE OF A. F. POOR, PEABODY.

Edward A. Maloon.

In the affairs of the great M. Robson Leather company, a leading spirit is Edward A. Maloon. He is the son of the late William Maloon, and was born and reared in the city of Salem. The elder Maloon made the tanning business his life work and was a member of the once well-known firm of Maloon & Harrington, whose works adjoined those of M. Robson, and who were in a certain sense partners of the latter almost from the time he first started in business, Mr. Maloon doing the tanning and Mr. Robson the currying of the stock purchased by both. The subject of this sketch began his acquirement of the details of the leather industry soon after the conclusion of school life. After starting in business for himself he continued his father's tannery, and for twenty-five years, more or less, was closely identified with Matthew Robson in doing the tanning of the leather curried at the Robson factory. The consolidation of the three concerns, making one of the largest, if not the largest, enterprise of the kind in the United States, was effected in 1894, and is dwelt upon at length elsewhere in this volume. Mr. Maloon is now manager of the hide department of the M. Robson Leather company, and serves upon the board of directors. By his long and extensive commercial experience, he has become one of the best-known leather men of the country, having business acquaintances everywhere. At home, he is known as a just and equitable employer and a thoroughly public-spirited citizen.

His home in Beverly is a fine one, worthy of an eminently successful man of affairs. Mr. Maloon is prominent socially, being a thirty-second degree Mason. He has been connected with the Salem Cadets since 1864, and for over twenty years has served as an officer. He is also an active member of the Beverly Historical society and the Salem club.

JOSEPH H. POOR, Manager Tannery Dept., M. Robson Leather Co.

Alvah H. Bigelow.

Alvah H. Bigelow began his services with Mr. Robson as a bookkeeper in 1880, and now has charge of the office work of the company. Mr. Bigelow is a native of Vermont, is a war veteran, and spent some years in the west, coming to Salem in 1879. He has a direct interest in the Robson company and holds a seat in the directorate. He resides on Federal street.

EDWARD A MALOON

Michael Kelly.

George J. Godsland.

ALVAH H. BIGELOW

GEORGE J. GODSLAND.

and offices at 114 Washington street, Salem, commenced business with a capital of $10,000, under a charter of the state of Massachusetts, dated January, 1882, this being the third electric lighting company incorporated in Massachusetts, Boston having the first and Springfield the second. Electric lighting was quite a novelty in those days, and the projectors of the company were its principal customers. Its operations were commenced in a small building in the "West Yard," between Essex and Church streets. The business grew more rapidly than had been anticipated, and the engine power was doubled in a few weeks. In January, 1883, the first negotiations looking to street lighting were begun, and after some time, five arc lamps of 2,000 candle power each were put in

to Peabody and continued there until four years ago, when a dissolution occurred, Mr. Kelly continuing at his present location in the old Riley factory on Pope's court, near the Robson plant. During busy seasons he employs fifty hands and makes a specialty of glazed dull and white nappa. The Morrill Leather Co., 45 High street, Boston, are his selling agents. Mr. Kelly's record in public affairs is of the best. Aside from his aldermanic duties, he has been for some time a member of the school board and has served as an overseer of the poor. Mr. Kelly was a candidate for alderman in 1895, being defeated by one vote in a large poll. He is a democrat, a member of Lynn lodge of Elks and Veragua council, Knights of Columbus.

Salem Electric Lighting Co.

The Salem Electric Lighting company, whose plant is located on Peabody street,

MICHAEL KELLY.

operation in the streets of the city. This number has since been increased to one hundred and eighty-five. Early in 1888 the necessity for further enlargements was urgent, and in September of that year, the Barley wharf property on Peabody street was purchased and the building of the present station at once begun. In the construction of this plant, an endeavor was made to construct not only the most economical and the best running station possible, but with a view of making it of sufficient capacity for many years to come, and there is ample power in reserve. At present the steam plant consists of eight horizontal tubular boilers, one engine of 160 horse power, two of 350 horse power each, and one of 500 horse power. The electric plant, which is located in the second story of the building, consists of 12 30-light and 1 50-light arc dynamos of 2,000 candle power each, five large alternating incandescent dynamos, three power generators and four direct current incandescent dynamos. There are at present in use throughout the city about 15,000 incandescent lamps, and 400 arc lamps in the street and business houses of the city and 625 incandescent lamps in street service. Besides the electricity necessary for the above purposes, an immense quantity is furnished daily for power, which is used extensively for driving machinery in the various manufactories about the city. The continual growth and success of the company from its inception has been due to the determined efforts of the management to supply the citizens of the city with the most up-to-date and desirable forms of illumination, and it will be seen that the Salem Electric Lighting company plays no small part in the commercial activity of the city, and it certainly adds to its advantages as a manufacturing and commercial centre by its production of light and power for manufacturing purposes. The capital of the company, at present $175,000, is owned principally by the

INTERIOR OF SALEM ELECTRIC LIGHTING CO. STATION.

citizens of Salem, and being a home institution, it is certainly entitled to the patronage and support of those citizens who require light or power, as its rates are as low as is consistent with first class service. The management of the company is as follows: Directors—President, Chas. H. Price, James F. Almy, George M. Harris, Benj. W. Currier, Zadoc A. Gallup, Jos. N. Peterson; treasurer, H. M. Batchelder; general manager, S. Fred Smith; superintendent, Alphamco Morrill.

pany at 295 Bridge street in this city. The corporation controlling the enterprise was formed August 29, 1892. Work upon the building was pushed rapidly and in the following month everything was in readiness for the reception of goods. The original building was a most substantial brick structure, four stories high, with a basement, its outer dimensions being 62x48.6 feet. In 1894 an addition of 60x48.6 feet became necessary and again in the summer of 1896, sixty feet more were

SALEM STORAGE WAREHOUSE, BRIDGE STREET.

Salem Storage Warehouse.

Within a very few years, comparatively, the idea of receiving goods for storage has developed into a great industry. In every business centre throughout the country, warehouses of this description have been erected, but it is safe to assert that very few, if any, of these structures are better equipped for high class business than is that of the Salem Storage Warehouse com-

added, making the present length 182 feet with a floor area of 45,000 square feet. The walls are twenty inches thick up to the first floor, for the next two stories sixteen inches thick and the last two are twelve inches. Of the general construction of the warehouse, too much cannot be said. It is as substantial and safe as could well have been devised. The timbering is the heaviest of any building in the city, and every precaution which the day affords has been taken to guard against fire. Each window is protected by swinging shutters which have been carefully tinned and are closed at night. The elevator well is tinned throughout and heavy shutters divide the three sections of the building. All stairways are enclosed in brick. But little sheathing is used and the rates quoted by the insurance men are the lowest in the entire city. At all seasons a most equitable and desirable temperature is maintained, and there is not the slightest danger of harm to costly articles or furniture, such as pianos, etc. For the handling of goods, every arrangement to secure convenience and safety has been taken. Business sent or received by rail is transferred direct, a spur track of the Boston & Maine system having been laid to the doors. A huge elevator transports goods to all parts of the building, being operated by a fifteen horse-power electric motor placed in the basement. The elevator is furnished with a safety clutch for cases of extreme necessity in the breaking of a cable, and is guaranteed automatic. An entire wagon and load can be easily raised to any floor. From the first the company has received the most encouraging support from the citizens of Salem and vicinity. Besides the increase in bulk, as shown by the additional space required, the quality of the business has steadily advanced and the value now represented will aggregate an immense sum. The policy of the company and the direct management of the warehouse is such as to command the confidence of the most exacting and the business is now firmly established. The three upper floors of the building are partitioned into rooms of various sizes, with locked doors, to allow the storage of furniture, etc. In turn, the heavier goods are upon the lower floor and in the basement. The construction is such as to withstand a weight of three hundred pounds to the square inch, a much greater test than could be brought upon it. Business firms are represented here, the moderate cost of storage more than offsetting the saving in insurance premiums. The company has been officered from the first as follows: President, L. F. Hunt; treasurer, E. B. Symonds; manager, E. B. Trumbull. These, with H. P. Smith, W. H. Trumbull and Howard P. Harris, constitute the board of directors. Visitors will be welcomed at all times and an inspection will well repay the time required.

JAMES E. TRASK.

James E. Trask.

The work done by James E. Trask in the line of roofing has acquired the reputation throughout the county and beyond, of being the best obtainable. He is a life-long resident of Salem and was born October 9, 1842, the son of James and Lucy (Pierce) Trask. His father was the second penny post of the city, serving from 1836 to 1862. The son was educated in the public schools and in early life worked at the grocery and coal business. At the breaking out of the civil war, Mr. Trask was learning the trade of a painter with the late John G. Felt. Intensely devoted to the Union cause, the young painter enlisted in Co. A, of the fiftieth Massachusetts, and served in the Department of the Gulf under Generals Butler and Banks, being on detached duty at

Baton Rouge for a large portion of the time. At the close of his first period of service, Mr. Trask re-enlisted and was finally discharged at Boston, August 15, 1864. He returned to Salem and finished his time with Mr. Felt, for whom he later worked as a journeyman. In 1871 he began business upon his own account on Derby, formerly Fish street, and in the early 80's moved to his present location on Bridge street. With the painting, roofing work had been done, and this latter branch of the business so increased that Mr. Trask concluded to give his entire time to the same. Several men are now employed, doing the highest grade metallic work about roofs, skylights, cornices, etc., also asphalt and gravel roofing. Mr. Trask is the originator and proprietor of Trask's Elastic Building Cement, a standard article for repairing leaks about roofs, for bedding slate and tiles and for pointing wood, stone, iron and brick work. He is a strong prohibitionist, a member of the Central Baptist church and of the standing committee. He is also connected with John H. Chipman, Jr., post 89, G. A. R., of Beverly, of Fraternity lodge, I. O. O. F., John Endicott lodge, A. O. U. W. and Ethan Allen council, O. U. A. M. January 12, 1869, Mr. Trask married Miss Annie C. Osborne, youngest daughter of the late Capt. John B. Osborne. He has three children and resides at 47 St. Peter street.

George P. Woodbury.

This resident of Salem is a son of Ezra Woodbury and descended from John Woodbury, one of the early settlers of the town who came here as far back as 1622. The subject of this sketch attended the public schools and learned his trade in the employ of his father, who was a contractor and builder before him. Having been engaged in that business for several years past, he has built many substantial structures in and about Salem, and employs several men. Within the past few years he has become interested in real estate, and besides erecting several houses for speculation, has opened and developed an important section of land which greatly improves the entire section. This property, which consists of about five acres, comprises an extension of Fairmount and Woodside streets, and what was two years ago but a field, is now possessed of comely and comfortable residences, the occupants of which enjoy all the modern improvements, such as water, gas and electric lights and sewerage. One of these extensions has already been accepted by the city, and when the further extensions are

GEORGE P. WOODBURY.

made, it is conceded that the city will also accept them as thoroughfares. In the development of this locality, Mr. Woodbury has shown himself to be possessed of rare judgment as to real estate values, for the territory he has opened up is growing rapidly and is destined to become an important and convenient residential section. Mr. Woodbury has served as treasurer of the Firemen's Relief association from its formation. He is also a past regent of the Royal Arcanum, and is connected with other organizations. Although not an office seeker, he has served on the

FAIRMOUNT STREET WITH RESIDENCE OF GEORGE P. WOODBURY IN DISTANCE.

republican city committee for a decade and was for fifteen years... [illegible]

J. Brown & Sons.

The business of this firm was [begun] by Jonathan Brown, father of the present senior member... [illegible] 1833... [illegible] Beverly. The younger men succeeded to... [illegible] 1875... with his sons Jonathan Jr. and George A. Brown, have been associated with him. In 1878 the Brown factory was destroyed by fire... [illegible] the manufactory was located at the corner of Lafayette and Dodge streets at this city. On Christmas night, 1883, the entire shoe factory at the centre of Marblehead was burned, the firm meeting with a total loss. A factory was secured at Danvers, removal being made after eighteen months to the present factory, the property of the Salem Building association, on Canal street.

The product is misses' and children's machine-sewed, standard-screw and Goodyear [illegible] of hand and [illegible] supplies, and is manufacturers of these [illegible]. J. Brown & Sons [are] the only [illegible] of various [illegible] of Boston, having [illegible] hundred and fifty hands [illegible] employment [illegible] this year. In [illegible] have been a [illegible] product which [illegible] in storage and the weekly payroll is $800. System [illegible] $5000. An army of fifty others [are] kept at work, but [illegible] absorbs the [illegible] of the factory. [illegible] the Boston [illegible] The eastern [illegible] and west [illegible] extending both north and south of [illegible] this country, the Pacific West Indies, and America, etc. Has been a life [illegible] for Seaman [illegible] etc. relations with employees have been such [illegible] most of them have [illegible] south social and city... [illegible] despite [illegible] a house full and successful business methods. The factory adds to the prosperity of the entire society.

SHOE FACTORY OF J. BROWN & SONS.

Danvers Bleachery and Dye Works.

Among the great enterprises of Essex county which have contributed in no small measure to the prosperity of Salem and its environs, probably none have achieved a more wide and excellent reputation than has the Danvers Bleachery and Dye Works. It is, in fact, a time-honored concern in the history of the county, having been established in 1847 by Theophilus W. Walker, Nathaniel Walker, and E. W. Upton. The Walker heirs have since inherited and most successfully carried on the business. The extensive plant is at present owned by Grant Walker and his sister Mrs. Oscar E. Iasagi, the former idea of the magnitude of the enterprises may be learned from the output, which is eighty tons per week, or 23,000,000 yards of cloth per annum. The class of goods handled comprises sheetings, shirtings, cambrics, muslins, sateens, silesias, window shades, table damask, covers and napkins in cotton and linen, towels, crashes, etc. The trade of the house extends throughout the New England and middle states, New York, Pennsylvania and the south, and is principally derived from mills and large commission houses. The Boston office of the concern is at 92 State street, and from that point the extensive operations of the house are conducted.

DANVERS BLEACHERY AND DYE WORKS.

being manager of the works and J. Howard Fallon, superintendent. The factories are located at the junction of Foster and Washington streets, Peabody, on the line of the South Reading branch of the Boston & Maine R. R. and consist of a main building measuring 450x60 feet, substantially constructed of brick and stone, and numerous other buildings which are necessary in conducting the business. The machinery embraces every modern device known to the trade, and the works have every facility for the successful carrying on of the business. Constant employment is given to about one hundred and sixty skilled operatives, of whom about twenty are women. An

Derby Estate.

A partial glimpse is here given of the famous Derby estate property, now owned by James F. Almy. The Derbys of old Salem in her commercial days were the original owners, and the title goes back into the dim past, till it knits the provincial and the colonial times together. The older inhabitants remember and often speak of the glory of the ancient demesne. A thousand live oaks flourished on the broad acres. The old manor house nestled among the shadows of trees of many sorts brought from the old world, and a hedge of English thorn shut in the wonderful

DERBY ESTATE, LAFAYETTE STREET FRONT

garden, its porters' lodge, gold-fish pond, hot-houses and box-lined walks, where often sauntered gladsome youths and maidens. But times change, and the branch of the Derby family owning this property became reduced to three elderly maiden ladies. They sold this beautiful estate in 1867 to a syndicate composed of Nathaniel Wiggin, Charles S. Clark and James F. Almy. Transformation began at once. The property was surveyed, streets graded, and fine homes arose among the trees and flowers. The magnificent new normal school, recently located south of the Derby estate, includes also a kindergarten and model graded school. As this school is under the patronage and supervision of the state of Massachusetts, it is a great inducement for young families to locate here, where they can secure such superior educational advantages for their children. The contemplated improvements of the well-known Loring farm in a suitable and artistic manner, will make the Derby estate, which lies between that property and the city proper, all the more desirable for the location of homes. The sanitary necessities, in connection with the Loring property, will demand a trunk sewer, via Canal street and through the river valley of the Derby estate, to Loring avenue, with which every street and house on that property can be readily and naturally connected. Other parts of this city have grown largely during the past twenty-five or thirty years, but upon the Derby estate property has been the greatest increase of homes. Ward 5 now contains nearly one-third of the population of Salem and the marked increase of taxable property there is something marvellous. The diversified character of the extensive property presents a great variety of locations, and the prices of the lots vary from the lowest in the city, upward. The proprietors, while careful in the choice of customers, are proceeding in a very liberal manner towards purchasers. House lots are sold on easy terms and advances made to builders, when desired. The new residence of James F. Almy, one of the finest in Salem, graces one of the Lafayette street

RESIDENCE OF JAMES F. ALMY, LAFAYETTE STREET.

JAMES F. ALMY.

WALTER K. BIGELOW.

lots. A new street has been graded on the site of the old mansion, and the new opened lots, modern so far as lots are now taken.

Almy, Bigelow & Washburn.

The business of Almy, Bigelow & Washburn was begun in 1858, in a room

at 178 or 150 Essex street, on the Bowker block. The block has not been remodeled, so that the little shop is no longer in existence. In 1900 the business was moved to the West block, occupying a store now, stock, one of the several stores into which that block was then divided. This was, perhaps, the first modern enterprise established in Salem, the new methods being thoroughly modern and the cash system most effective. Before that time was usual to give six months credit to anyone.

CALVIN R. WASHBURN.

E. AUGUSTUS ANNABLE.

STORE ALMY, BIGELOW & WASHBURN, ESSEX STREET, PROPOSED NEW FRONT.

or a year's time and sell them on a credit of one year, and as much longer as the debtor was inclined to demand. It was the new method that gave the business its impetus, and it was its opportunity to enlarge which has enabled the firm to attain its present growth and influence. When the firm came to its present quarters there were nineteen distinct business enterprises within the confines of the estate. There are now but two tenants besides the great firm. The premises have been enlarged on twelve different occasions within the last seven years for the benefit of this thrifty house and the area occupied for business purposes on this property by this firm is now 75,000 square feet. It is understood that additional room is again necessary, and a plan is now in contemplation which, if carried out, will provide one of the largest stores in New England outside of Boston. It will not only be beautiful internally and externally, but arranged with every modern device for the needs of this progressive firm. This is a great department store. It is really a multitude of complete stores in one. The needs of the people can be thoroughly supplied there in articles of the best quality, highest utility, always modern and just what you want, at prices so reasonable that when people get in the habit of going there they continue to go. There is not space in this article to set forth systematically or in detail the operations and benefits of this great enterprise. One must visit it and spend an hour in the labyrinth of its extensive departments, halls, rooms and alcoves, stored with the product of many nations, to realize its magnitude. It not only employs a great force of helpers in the distribution of merchandise, but there is also a multitude of mechanics and artisans occupied in the outside shops and warehouses. It has long been conceded that the firm of Almy, Bigelow & Washburn do a larger business in proportion to the population of its city than any other like concern in the United States. It is not, perhaps, too much to say that in the manifestations of their business methods this firm is a help to the community. It is a training school for young people, affording a better education than any school of theory. Its systematic methods of promotion give an opportunity to a child coming from the humblest home to obtain the highest position and the best salary the business affords. It is particularly a school for girls; and there are scores of women in Salem and elsewhere who have married from this store, and who will say frankly that the discipline had while in the employment of this firm has been of incalculable benefit in fitting them for the duties of life. The members of the firm all sprang from plain people, and their early lives were struggles with poverty which gave them self-reliance. They decline to have their history written, and only desire to have it understood that their great business enterprise is not only to make money, but to be of service to the public. Almy, Bigelow & Washburn take special interest in their mail order department, which has grown through the influence of summer visitors to Salem and vicinity who were pleased to continue patronage with them after they return to their permanent homes. Indeed it is now so important that they have re-organized their mail order department on a comprehensive scale. Their trade reaches everywhere. They pay the carriage on all parcels ordered by mail to the nearest post or express office anywhere in the United States. Samples of all goods are sent post paid on application.

W. G. Webber & Co.

This business was established in September, 1885, by the present firm and has since continued an honorable name and a veritable trade mark to all purchasers of reliable dry goods. Mr. Webber is a splendid organizer and perfect system and correct mercantile methods have ever characterized this great establishment, which is representative of what the trade has become under the stimulating influences of practically unlimited resources, perfect facilities and unremitting energy and enterprise. The premises occupied consist of the three-story building, 238-240 Essex street and 94-96 Washington street, which is elegantly fitted with large plate glass windows, electric lights and all

WILLIAM G. WEBBER.

WILLIAM B. MANSFIELD.

the latest improvements in interior decorations. This is essentially a dry goods store, and while carpets and shoes are kept under the same roof, the firm claims to do the largest dry goods business in the city. The stock comprises staple and fancy dry goods, hosiery, linens, millinery,

WILLIAM G. WEBBER & CO.
Essex Street front.

WILLIAM G. WEBBER & CO.,
Washington Street front.

MILLINERY DEPT. WM. G. WEBBER & CO.

the season, and the trade of the house extends over an immense territory, a large mail order business being done. The members of the firm are recognized authorities in the trade, and constantly buying to meet special demands of their patrons. They import direct many of their staple and fancy goods, and have an agent in Paris who attends to the purchase and selection of the latest Parisian novelties, which are shown in the various departments of the store, always in advance of the city. Mr. Webber was born in North Beverly, and is

dress goods in all the latest and finished effects, silks, satins, velvets, white goods, laces, gloves, cloaks, costumes, etc. A large stock of carpets, boots, shoes, and gents' shoes is also carried. Quality has ever been the first consideration throughout this enormous stock, while the prices are marvelously low, considering the exceptionally high character of the goods. The trade of the house has grown steadily since its inception. It is at present one of the largest in the dry goods line outside of Boston. From 100 to 150 clerks are employed in the various departments, according to the

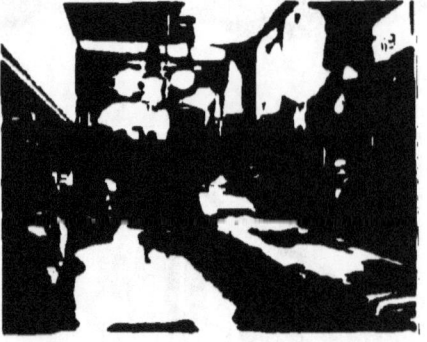

DRESS GOODS DEPARTMENT WM. G. WEBBER & CO.

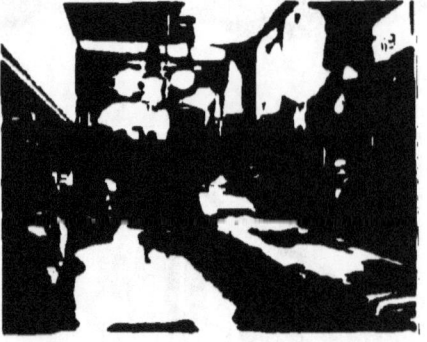

RESIDENCE WM. G. WEBBER, LAFAYETTE ST.

ness mastering its every detail and by his strict integrity and capability was ultimately placed in a position of trust, subsequently being admitted to partnership. He is most highly esteemed in business and social circles.

Frank A. Wendell.

Frank A. Wendell, who has his main store in the Kinsman block, 79 Washington street, controls the largest plumbing business in the entire county, and with the fine display of the latest and most approved sanitary appliances, the establishment is one of the leaders of its kind in all New England. Mr. Wendell has not reached his present position without a heroic effort, but he may truly claim to be, in every respect, a self-made man. He was born in Portsmouth, N. H., January 29, 1854, and

FRANK A. WENDELL.

graduated from the high school at the age of fifteen. He entered the employ of the United States government at the Kittery, Maine, navy yard and served four years, graduating as a journeyman plumber in 1871. Mr. Wendell removed to Salem and at first was employed by Daniel F. Staten. Upon the death of the latter, Mr. Wendell began business for himself at 7 Crombie street, moving about a year later to 8 North st., with a storehouse at 7 St. Peter street. For his rapidly increasing trade, larger quarters became a necessity and the present fine location was secured. It was at this stand that Mr. Wendell started an innovation in the business—the fitting up of an elaborate display of sanitary plumbing, showing the actual workings. In the spring of 1896 the store at Watertown was

RESIDENCE OF FRANK A. WENDELL.

F. A. WENDELL'S SALEM STORE.

founded, followed a little later by a similar enterprise at Beverly, both stores being fitted with the same care and detail as the parent establishment on Washington street. A better idea of the magnitude of the business may be had when it is known that forty-five persons are now employed to...

building, Watertown, Naumkeag, Neal and Newhall, and Manning blocks and the new residences of James F. Almy and J. M. Parsons, Salem, and the magnificent new station of the Boston & Maine railroad at Beverly. Mr. Wendell is prominent socially, being a member of the Odd Fellows, United Workmen, Royal Arcanum, and American Mechanics. He is a large real estate owner. Mr. F. A. Ober, the manager of the branch stores, has been connected with the business for the past eight years, commencing as bookkeeper in 1890, gradually mastering all the metres whole career, in this capacity, until the increasing territory covered compelled the employment of clerical assistance at each store, when he was promoted to his present position, which he has filled with fidelity and credit. William A. Webber, formerly of the firm of William A. Webber & Co., is foreman at Beverly, John F. Dixon, formerly of the firm of Creswell and Dixon, holding a similar position at Watertown.

W. C. Packard Furniture and Carpet Company.

The above firm can justly claim the distinction of being the oldest in the line of...

INTERIOR F. A. WENDELL'S SALEM STORE.

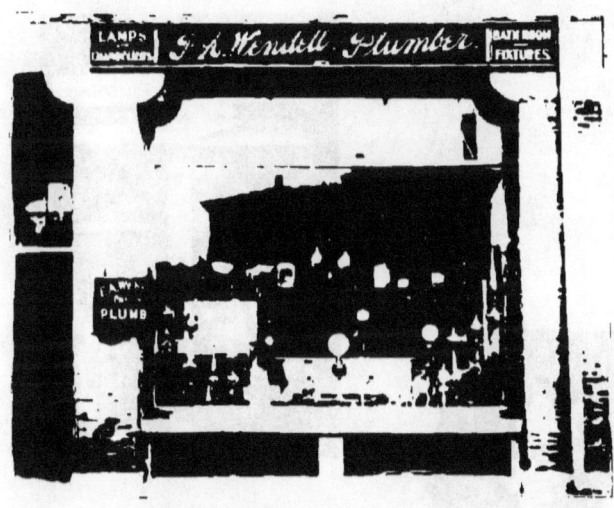

F. A. WENDELL'S BEVERLY STORE.

ing opened up a vista of elegance in housekeeping, which, until its advent, had not been dreamed of. Walter C. Packard, the founder of this house, was born in Boston in 1842, and received his education in the public and high schools of that city, upon leaving which he entered into partnership with his father under the style of P. F. Packard & Sons. Mr. Packard remained in the firm for fifteen years, mastering every detail of the furniture business. In 1872 he came to Salem and began in the same line at the present store, corner of Essex and Crombie streets, occupying but two floors. The premises were burned out in January 1881, and for a time business was carried on in Mechanic hall, pending the re-building of the entire block, which has since been occupied by the concern. The enterprise was incorporated in 1886 under the present style, George F. Roach of George F. Roach & Co., Boston, being chosen president and Mr. Packard acting as sole manager and treasurer of the company. The present location comprises ten

INTERIOR F. A. WENDELL'S BEVERLY STORE.

floors, each 125 feet deep, lighted by electricity and heated by steam throughout. A magnificent and costly stock is carried, consisting of furniture, carpets, house furnishing goods, draperies, upholstered goods, stoves, ranges, lamps, bric-à-brac, etc. High grade bicycles are also handled. Everything is selected with care and judgment and close inspection, the stock can be said to be one of the largest and most complete in the state, outside of the metropolis. The old West Church is used as storehouse and there are also

F. A. WENDELL'S WATERTOWN STORE.

FRED A. OBER.

of all sorts besides a large and increasing stock. This concern has extensive stores at the south, the successors of a famous and well known house. The patrons of Messrs. Ober Brothers, to which reference is now being made, occupy three spacious floors, carrying a most complete and choice stock and dealing in all kinds of goods. Various departments exist under the able management of Mr. F. A. Ober. In fact this enterprising business man is esteemed everywhere.

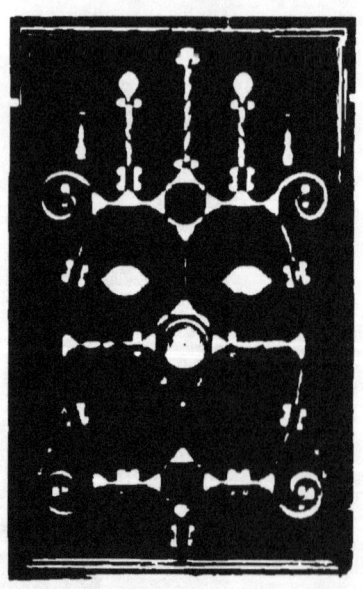

SPECIMEN PLUMBING WORK OF F. A. WENDELL.

Essex House.

A marvellous effect in transformation was presented to the citizens of Salem in March, 1897, at which time the remodelled Essex house was opened for the reception of guests under the management of H. W. Fiske. A hostelry upon this site has been one of the landmarks of the city for decades, but the general style of entertainment was not, until recently, fully worthy of the leading hotel in a city of the size and importance of Salem. The Essex house of today, however, is a most happy and harmonious blending of the comfort and elegance of the new with the quaintness and historic interest of the former days. In furnishings and equipment the place would reflect credit upon a much larger community, while no city of Salem's size can show a finer hotel.

WALTER C. PACKARD.

first class goods. Mr. Packard is one of Salem's most substantial and enterprising business men and has been active in all matters pertaining to the prosperity of the city.

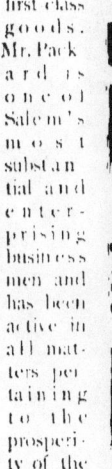

INTERIOR W. C. PACKARD FURNITURE AND CARPET CO.'S STORE.

With the additional room secured at the time of the refitting, there are now seventy-two sleeping apartments, besides the office, parlors, reception rooms, dining halls, etc., over 30,000 square feet of floor space being devoted to its uses. The main entrance on Essex street, in the heart of the retail section, is most pleasingly connected with the new style, opening directly from a large and comfortable lobby. The rooms throughout the hotel are spacious and the furnishings are of the choicest designs. A dainty private dining room is one main floor. The furnishings of the parlors and sleeping rooms are in the best of taste, the latter systematically arranged, and most of the rooms being connecting with bath rooms. The house is heated by steam and lighted by electricity and gas throughout.

INTERIOR ESSEX HOUSE DINING ROOM

CHARLES H. ODELL.

W. HARDY DAYTON.

steamship and railroad ticket office and banking agency at 252 Essex street for the sale of tourist, European and coastwise steamer tickets and for issuing drafts and letters of credit on foreign monetary centres. He is agent for the principal steamship and railroad lines and is an authority on all matters pertaining to travel, either at home or abroad. As local agent for the Cheque bank of London, Knauth, Nachod & Kuhne, bankers, New York, the Massachusetts National Bank, Boston, and the Cunard Steamship company, he is enabled to furnish the travelling public with drafts on the principal commercial cities of the eastern & western hemispheres, or with money orders or cheques payable on demand in the United States or in any city of the world, a convenience which obviates the necessity of identification at foreign banks with its attendant vexatious delays, expense, and inconvenience. Mr. Dayton is also a real estate and insurance broker, negotiates loans on approved security and represents several of the strongest fire, life, accident and baggage insurance companies. He is prominent in secret societies and is an enterprising and successful business man in his chosen lines.

Fred H. Fowler.

One of the choicest stocks of meats, provisions and groceries to be found in this section is constantly on hand at the store of Fred H. Fowler, 13 North street. The provision business at this location was begun by Warren G. Upton in 1889, and from the most unpretentious beginnings became, in a very short time, a decided and permanent success. In 1892, the store passed into the hands of Fowler & Whelton, so continuing until the summer of 1897, when Mr. Fowler assumed the full proprietorship. The market is a most commodious one, an addition of fifteen feet having been built lately, making the dimensions at present 55x17. Mr. Fowler prides himself upon the especially high grade of fresh meat always carried in stock and his trade in this line is of the best. Fresh vegetables are received each morning, largely from the farms of A. P. Knapp and O. F. Newhall at Peabody. Another specialty is the Watch brand of tomatoes canned expressly for Mr. Fowler's trade and having the reputation of being the very finest obtainable. Standard groceries, such as flour, teas and

FRED H. FOWLER.

coffees, fancy crackers and butter, can also be supplied in any quantity at the lowest consistent prices. Orders for fresh fish can be promptly filled, the Boston fish market being closely connected with Mr. Fowler's store. Four teams are in constant use and the business is having a most healthy growth. The proprietor is a life long resident of Salem and, with the

tion at the Dirigo Business College where he displayed such marked ability that he was offered and accepted a position on the staff of teachers, holding the position for three years. He then engaged in the photographic business which he conducted for two years most successfully in his native town and then removed to Lewiston, where he remained one year. In 1885, Mr. Hus-

WILLIAM G. HUSSEY.

FRANK H. SARGENT.

INTERIOR APPLETON HOUSE, BROOKLINE. WORK OF F. H. SARGENT.

magnificent structure for C. B. Appleton of Brookline, an exact model of one of the most attractive buildings upon the World's Fair grounds at Chicago in 1893, and of which an interior view is here given. The frame of the building is of wood, metal lathed and covered with several coats of Portland cement. Both exterior and interior furnished numerous opportunities for the exercise of the greatest skill and ingenuity, both of which were abundantly supplied by Mr. Sargent and his expert force. Since an early age, Mr. Sargent has been active in religious work, is now a deacon of the South Congregational church, for ten consecutive years has been superintendent of the Sunday school, and is a director in the Salem Y. M. C. A. He joined Cumberland lodge of Odd Fellows at Bridgeton, Me., in 1874, and was a charter member of Norway lodge and Widdey encampment, I. O. O. F., of Norway. His membership has been transferred to Essex lodge and Naumkeag encampment of Salem. He is also a member of John Endicott lodge, A. O. U. W. Although repeatedly urged to take public office, Mr. Sargent has declined to do so.

L. E. Millea.

L. E. Millea, heating and building engineer and sanitary expert, with place of business at 154 Washington street, has had long experience, having been in the business since 1868; and he is considered an authority on all matters pertaining to heating and sanitation. He was born in Ireland, coming to this city when a child, and was educated in the public and private schools of Salem and Peabody, acquiring a thorough scientific education, which has stood him in good stead in his chosen vocation and is the basis of his success as an expert. He is the inventor and manufacturer of the "Hathorne House Heater," an apparatus made on new lines, in a thoroughly scientific manner, which ensures the best results for the least expense. Mr. Millea has always taken a lively interest in public affairs, having served in the city council, school committee and board of park commissioners. He also belongs to many associations in the city, including the board of trade, master builders association and a number of insurance organizations. His customers are the best, and his work may be

L. E. MILLEA.

WILLIAM A. CLEVELAND.

found in the most palatial of the private residences and other fine structures throughout Essex county. All who are looking for the safest and best work, rather than for the cheapest, naturally turn to Mr. Millea, who has a high reputation for the best material and execution at the lowest living prices.

William A. Cleveland.

One of the most important and reliable representatives of the wholesale produce commission trade of Essex county is the old established and leading house of W. A. Cleveland, which was established fifteen years ago by its present proprietor, and has since developed a trade that has few equals either in extent of operations or scope of territory covered in this section. The facilities of the house are of the most advanced character, well adapted for the handling of stock with promptitude and despatch. Mr. Cleveland enjoys close relations with producers and shippers and is constantly in receipt of choice consignments in car load lots, which are promptly distributed to the trade throughout this and adjoining cities. Store houses are maintained at Houlton and Presque Isle, Me., and at Atlanta, N. Y., and all the operations of the house are conducted under the supervision of the proprietor, whose large experience, ample resources and advanced methods insure the most satisfactory relations with both shippers and customers. Mr. Cleveland was born in Camden, Me., in 1840, receiving his education in the public schools. In his early manhood he went to sea, attaining the rank of mate, but tiring of the life, he engaged in his present line of business in Boston, coming to Salem fifteen years ago. In 1894 he was elected to represent Ward 5 in the common council, and re-elected the following year. He has always taken an active personal interest in public affairs, and has served with distinction under the present city government on the

C. H. PHIPPEN.

committees on streets, bridges and sewers, public instruction, printing, fuel and street lighting, and water works. He was elected an alderman in 1896. Mr. Cleveland has always been recognized as a careful, conservative but enterprising business man, and his natural faculties make him a valuable official in the position he now occupies, and will earn for him promotion to broader usefulness in political life in the future.

C. H. Phippen.

The oldest established plumbing business in Salem is that operated by Charles H. Phippen at 19 St. Peter street. Mr. Phippen is a native of Salem and was born in 1838. After being educated in the Salem public schools, he learned his trade as a plumber from the late Francis P. Goss, whose shop was then on St. Peter street, and who was widely known in the old days as a capable and reliable master plumber. After obtaining a thorough knowledge of all the practical details of the business, Mr. Phippen, in 1868, started for himself. For nearly thirty years the business has flourished and developed under his continuous management. The first shop was on Boston street, but in January, 1896, improved quarters were taken in a more central location at 19 St. Peter street, close to the spot where the proprietor learned his trade. At this place he conducts a general plumbing business, which has gained a wide reputation. Large or small contracts are taken, and no work is slighted, everything being done with painstaking attention, and every effort made for durable and serviceable results. The proprietor is conservative in his methods. He has wisely concentrated his efforts upon first-class plumbing consisting of piping for water, gas and drainage purposes exclusively. Perhaps no man in the city understands his business better than Mr. Phippen; and the quality of his work is his best advertisement. He has done the plumbing work on many of the best business and residential structures in Essex county. A full line of sanitary appliances is always carried. Fred T. Phippen, his son, ably assists him and has an interest in the business.

L. E. STOVER.

GEORGE J. KERR.

Stover & Kerr.

The store at 197 Essex street occupied by the above firm has been a clothing store for over half a century and is a landmark in the business of the city. The present proprietors, L. E. Stover and George J. Kerr, assumed control of it five years ago, and by unremitting energy, coupled with really first class goods, have built up a most enviable reputation as clothiers and men's outfitters. Their stock is replete with clothing ready to wear, each garment being equally as good as custom-made work, and an excellent assortment of furnishing goods, shirts, collars, neckwear, etc., in all the leading and most fashionable styles. Mr. Stover was born in Newburyport, but has resided nearly all his life in Salem. Mr. Kerr was born in Boston, April 7, 1851, but was located in Manchester-by-the-Sea and has been in Salem twenty-seven years. Both the partners are prominent in the secret societies, being members of the Masonic order, I. O. O. F., A. O. U. W., and Red Men. They are enterprising and progressive business men and their future success is assured.

John L. Dickinson.

Beyond doubt, the largest individual horse dealer in Essex county is John L. Dickinson of Salem. By his extensive and straightforward dealings, he has become acquainted with business men scattered over a large area. The volume of his trade now aggregates thousands of dollars per annum. A native of Ipswich, he was educated in that town, graduating from the high school with the class of '72. He engaged in general trading until 1877, when he removed to Rockport, at first running a stage line from Rockport depot to Pigeon Cove and later bought and managed a livery stable. The next nine years were spent in his native town, where he resumed trading. In April, 1890, Mr. Dickinson opened a livery and general horse business at 10 Beacon street, Salem, and in December, 1896, he removed to his present location at 37 Bridge street. Besides accommodating forty horses, 7,500 square feet are set aside as a carriage repository and at all seasons of the year stock is kept moving. The proprietor makes frequent trips to the west, in search of the best which that market affords in the line of horse flesh and the success of his missions can be attested by many who have obtained valuable animals from among the selections. Mr. Dickinson married in 1880 and has two children. In the midst of pressing business cares, he finds time for social connections, being a member of Jerusalem senate, K. A. E. O., Naumkeag tribe of Red Men and Francis Higginson colony, U. O. P. F. He is a member of the national executive committee of the Carriage and Harness Dealers' ass'n.

SALEM HORSE AND CARRIAGE MART.

Salem and South Danvers Oil Co.

The plant of the Salem and South Danvers oil company is located at 43-53 Mason street and covers an area of over 50,000 square feet. The business was established in 1855, the works being devastated by fire in 1887, but they have since been rebuilt in a more substantial manner, and the latest improved machinery added, making them the most complete establishment of the kind in New England. The products consist principally of rosin oil, paraffine oils, lubricating, cylinder and machinery oils, curriers' grease, refining rosin and producing oil from it, used in printer's ink, leather blacking, ship chandlers' bright varnish, etc. The transportation facilities of the house are excellent and their products are in general use throughout the United States, while they enjoy the distinction of being the only house in New England making rosin oil. Large quantities of fish oils, sulphuric, nitric and muriatic acids are handled and the trade in this line is rapidly increasing. About 1,000 barrels of currier's grease, together with oils, are produced monthly, and twenty skilled workmen are employed. The products of the house have attained an excellent reputation in the trade and are all of standard merit. The officers of the company are R. H. Brown, president, F. P. Symonds, secretary and treasurer.

THE SALEM CHEMICAL AND SUPPLY CO.

with office at 43 Mason street and laboratory on Walter street, is doing a large and steadily increasing business. In 1891 the company commenced bottling petroleum jelly and ammonia in a room about twelve feet square on Mason street. The goods found a ready sale and it was soon necessary to look for larger quarters. A building 40x60 was secured on Walter street, and there the company began the manufacture of toilet waters, flavoring extracts, etc., and gradually adding a line of essential oils and druggists' supplies. The business has steadily increased through the recent financial depression, and it has been found necessary to enlarge several times. The company now occupies over 13,000 square feet of floor space and stands at the head in its line, both as to quality and amount of goods handled. The daily shipments are from 300 to 1,000 dozen of bottled goods and about an equal amount in bulk. A large business is also done in prescription bottles and corks and a larger stock is carried in this line than by a majority of jobbers who confine themselves to the bottling business alone. The goods are sold principally in New England and New York, although orders from the west and south are frequent. H. W. Boyd is manager of the company, F. P. Symonds acting as treasurer.

THE SALEM WASTE COMPANY

was established in 1891 and its inception was due to the ever growing demands for cotton waste, so essential for the cleaning of machinery. The plant is a well equipped one, having exceptionally good advantages for the economical treatment of the raw material and has a capacity of five tons of waste per day, which is readily sold to jobbers throughout New England. The industry has thrived from the commencement and its business is annually increasing. The works are at 43 Mason street.

WORKS SALEM AND SOUTH DANVERS OIL CO.

Thomas G. Pinnock.

The name of Pinnock has been identified with the slate roofing business in Salem since 1857, when Thomas Pinnock, father of the subject of this sketch, opened a shop on Peabody street, removing in 1862 to the present premises on Dodge street. His enterprise enjoys the distinction of being the oldest in the building line in Salem and has always enjoyed an excellent reputation on account of the superior manner in which every contract is carried out. In 1872, Thomas G. Pinnock was admitted to partnership with his father, the firm being Thomas Pinnock & Son until 1878, when Thomas G. Pinnock assumed complete control of, and has since most successfully conducted it. Among the contracts carried out may be mentioned the roofing of the court

RESIDENCE OF THOMAS O. PINNOCK.

houses, Wesley chapel, the State Normal school and nine public school buildings in Salem; while in Gloucester, Mr. Pinnock has roofed the Baptist church, high school and seven public school houses, also the Manchester public library. Born at Lowell, Mass., in 1851, Mr. Pinnock came to Salem in 1857 and attended the public schools here. In business circles he is highly esteemed and is a prominent member of several societies, both secret and fraternal.

Nathaniel Abbott.

For the past forty-five years Nathaniel Abbott has been closely identified with the commercial progress of Salem and, although he has never aspired to nor accepted a public office, he has always taken a deep interest in all matters pertaining to the city's welfare and advancement. Born in Shapleigh, Me., in 1828, he learned the tanning and currying business in his youth and followed it for three years, when he removed to Danvers and engaged in the livery business, subsequently removing to Salem and taking up the wholesale fish business at Phillps' wharf. Mr. Abbott formed a partnership with Moses C. Reynolds fifteen years later, and has since been actively engaged in the wholesale country produce business and the sale of horses, having stables at 52 Charter street and offices and storehouses at 24 Front street. Upon the death of Mr. Reynolds nineteen years ago, his son, Henry Reynolds, was admitted to and still remains in the firm, the style being as formerly, Abbott & Reynolds. Mr. Abbott has been connected with the Y. M. C. A. for many years and is also a member of the Essex Institute and of the Grand Army. His business methods have always been of the highest character and the firm's standing is exceptionally good. Mr. Abbott is known as one of the substantial citizens of the community.

W. S. MACKINTIRE & CO.'S SALEM IRON FOUNDRY.

NATHANIEL ABBOTT.

William F. M. Collins.

William F. M. Collins was born in Salem, January 24, 1855, receiving his education in the public and private schools of his native city. He studied law in the office of Wm. P. Upham, with Jairus W. Perry and Leverett S. Tuckerman, being admitted to the Essex County bar, September 19, 1877. He began practice for himself the same year, making a specialty of real estate property, conveyancing, and probate law, upon which he is a recognized authority. He has been public administrator for a number of years and was a member of the common council in 1878, '79 and '80, being

WILLIAM H. HUNT.

elected clerk of the council in January, 1884, a position which he has since most acceptably filled.

William H. Hunt.

Among the most progressive of the younger business men of the city is William H. Hunt, architect and practical superintendent, with offices in the Naumkeag building of which he was the first tenant. Previously, Mr. Hunt had been located at Beverly. He was born at Concord, N. H., but

WILLIAM F. M. COLLINS.

for several years has done a large business in his line throughout this section, making a specialty of the planning of dwelling houses of the most approved and modern construction, although his experience has ranged through all departments of the profession. Besides the numerous examples of his work in this city, Mr. Hunt has had large employment in Beverly, Peabody, Danvers, Revere, Malden, and several other cities and towns, securing contracts for buildings of almost every description in competition with many competitors. In the line of dwellings, Mr. Hunt has obtained an enviable reputation in the designing of structures that are at once original and tasty, yet without affectation. He has also built a large number of houses for investment, which have met with a ready sale and in this branch Mr. Hunt has been conspicuously successful. He is also a thoroughly practical man as regards the estimates and supervision of new buildings, having a complete knowledge of the markets, and technicalities of the trade.

William A. Swan & Co.

William A. Swan, who conducts a tailoring business in the Price block, Essex street, under the firm name of William A. Swan & Co., has resided in Salem for the past sixteen years, having an extensive custom among those desiring work of the highest grade. Mr. Swan removed with his parents from his native state of Ohio in 1866, to Camden, Me., being at that time nine years old. He began to learn his trade at Camden in 1870, remaining there for the succeeding six years, and later worked in Rockland at the same business. Mr. Swan learned the art of cutting with Osborne & Hale of Boston, immediately after settling in this city. He was at first associated with H. B. Wilmot, the location being on Essex street, opposite the present store. In 1882, in company with R. A. Mackenzie Mr. Swan engaged the quarters he now occupies, the firm style being Mackenzie & Swan, and the latter has conducted the business alone since the death of Mr. Mackenzie in 1889. The work rooms are on the top floor of the building in which the store is located. Personal attention is given to all the details of garment making and satisfaction is guaranteed. Mr. Swan is a member of the Honorary Cadets and of John Endicott lodge, Ancient Order of United Workmen of this city.

INTERIOR W. A. SWAN'S TAILORING ESTABLISHMENT

Holyoke Mutual Fire Insurance Co.

This is by far the largest of the several insurance enterprises having headquarters in this city. By its name it perpetuates the memory of Dr. E. A. Holyoke, a noted physician of Salem and the first president of the Massachusetts Medical society, who died March 31, 1829, at that time having spanned seven months over a century of life. Organized March 27, 1843, the company began business May 14, of the same year. John S. Williams was chosen as the first president and he served until October, 1848. He was succeeded by Augustus Story, who filled the position for thirty-four years. Thomas H. Johnson acted as president pro tem from October, 1882, until January, 1883, Alfred A. Abbott assuming the presidency at the latter date and continuing to November, 1884. Since that time, Charles H. Price, the present incumbent, has performed the duties of this office. Since January, 1885, Thomas H. Johnson has served as vice president and as general manager of the company since 1882. The first secretary was John T. Burnham, who was succeeded in November, 1861, by Thomas H. Johnson. Upon the latter's promotion to the vice presidency in 1885, Walter L. Harris was chosen and still continues as secretary. President Story acted as treasurer from the organization of the company up to October, 1882, followed by Joseph O. Proctor, with a term extending to January, 1885. For the past twelve years, Thomas H. Johnson has cared for the finances, in connection with his duties as vice president. Walter L. Harris, Frank T. Dalrymple and Louis O. Johnson have, in turn, held the assistant secretaryship. Business was conducted upon the assessment plan until 1853, when the ordinary premium policy, as practised by nearly all the large insurance companies, was adopted. The Holyoke company is now represented by one hundred and seventy agents, risks being restricted to the states of Maine, Massachusetts, Rhode Island and Connecticut. The losses paid aggregate $1,979,917, policies to the amount of $42,000,000 now being in force. For losses arising from the great Portland fire of 1866, $129,000 was paid, and following the Boston catastrophe of six years later, $210,000 was promptly forwarded as the Holyoke's share in repairing the enormous waste wrought at that time. In February, 1873, the company acquired a guarantee capital of $100,000, as a further protection to its policy holders. Cash assets of $850,000 are available, the liabilities, including capital, amounting to $400,000. A surplus of $450,000 net, or, including capital of $550,000 so far as policy holders are concerned, has accrued. The home office is in a fine three-story building owned by the company and situated in the heart of the business section of the city. Upon the ground floor are also the rooms of the Salem National bank, the second and third floors being used for office and club purposes. The present directors are, Charles H. Price, B. F. Fabens, Thomas H. Johnson, J. T. Mahoney, Daniel Low, A. L. Huntington and H. M. Batchelder of Salem, George R. Harris, Brookline, G. A. Tapley, Danvers, and F. H. Appleton, Peabody. As townsmen and personal acquaintances of the men who have made the Holyoke Mutual Fire Insurance company the extensive and successful institution it is today, the citizens of Salem of the past and present have been given an object lesson as to the worthy purposes and honorable methods characteristic of great enterprises of this kind, now so necessary an adjunct to the fullest commercial and domestic security. During the entire history of the company, every dollar of loss honestly suffered by any policy-holder has been promptly and fully replaced upon the presentation of the reasonable proof required in such cases. Heavy at times though the blows may have been, no permanent harm has been done and the Holyoke has gone on, from success to success, and was never accorded more encouraging support, more loyal service or a greater share of general prosperity than at the present day. As firmly as the reputation of the city is established, so is that of the Holyoke Mutual Fire Insurance company, making its headquarters and home office in Salem.

JOHN C. MACDONALD.

J. C. Macdonald & Co.

Without question the largest tailoring business in the city of Salem is that done by John C. Macdonald under the firm name of John C. Macdonald & Co., the location being on the second floor of the Northey building, corner of Essex and Washington Sts. Mr. Macdonald was born at Springton, P. E. I., April 22, 1860, of Scotch descent, his parents being among the earliest Scotch to remove to Prince Edward Island. He attended the public schools of his native place, and in 1874 began a five years apprenticeship with Angus Macswann, a prominent tailor still doing business at Summerside, P. E. I. In July, 1879, Mr. Macdonald entered the famous cutting school of J. J. Mitchell & Co., New York, for the purpose of perfecting his training. After his graduation, he removed to Boston, and, although hardly twenty years of age, acted for three years as cutter and manager for the large firm of John Philips & Co., formerly the Phelps, Shuman Co. The next two and one-half years were spent with Charles Green & Co., as head cutter and designer. In 1888, Mr. Macdonald accepted an offer to manage the custom department of Almy, Bigelow & Washburn's store, remaining here until 1890, when he began manufacturing upon his own account in the Mavins building, Essex street. In August, 1894, he removed to his present commodious and elegant rooms in the Northey building. Here Mr. Macdonald gives his personal

INTERIOR J. C. MACDONALD & CO.'S TAILORING PARLORS.

attention to the designing and cutting of all the patterns, assisted by Edward McKinnon. The manufacturing department is at 5 Higginson square, connected by a private telephone line. An average force of twenty-five hands is employed. Tailoring work is done for both ladies and gentlemen, over one-half of which is for out-of-town trade, including a large amount for Boston parties. The stock of woolens, worsteds, etc., constantly on hand is, like the work done, of the highest grade. Mr. Macdonald is a direct importer from the textile centres of Peebles, Scotland, and Huddersfield, England. The best German and domestic cloths are also handled. Mr. Macdonald is affiliated with all the Masonic bodies of both the York and Scottish rites in the city, also with Allepo Temple of the Mystic Shrine, Boston. He was the first Chief of Clan Wallace, O. S. C., is a member of the grand and royal grand bodies of the Order of Scottish clans, of Lynn lodge of Elks, of several local clubs, and is president of the Wallace Golf club. In February, 1892, Mr. Macdonald married Mrs. Anstice Poole of Peabody. He has two children and resides at 14 Leach street.

Warren Page.

Warren Page is the senior member of the firm of Warren Page & Co., manufacturers of shoe counters, with factory on Dodge street court. He was born at Newfield, Me., and is the son of Jacob Page, one of the oldest residents of that town. His early days were spent upon the farm and at the district school. Leaving home at the age of sixteen, Mr. Page at first located in Lowell and soon after came to Salem. He secured a position as clerk in a Front street store, and later, with only energy and brains as capital, began the counter manufacturing business in a small room on Margin street, employing one boy, the payment of whose salary often proved a matter of embarrassment. In five years, Mr. Page admitted his brother Mager to the concern, where he still remains. In 1882 a small factory was built on Dodge street court, and in 1885 another adjoining it. Soon the Page business necessitated taking a portion of this structure, also, and in 1894 the entire space of two substantial three-story buildings was demanded. The concern is the largest of its kind in the country and in busy

WARREN PAGE.

MR. AND MRS. ALPHONSE J. B. MOUTHUY.

seasons employs 175 hands. All grades, sizes and kinds of counters are turned out in immense quantities, averaging fifty barrels or 50,000 pairs per day. The equipment and machinery are most complete and modern and the trade is largely through the New England states. Mr. Page has the retiring, domestic tastes usually found in a successful man of business who owes his triumph to his own efforts. He is one of the best known men in his line in the country, but has always frowned upon any endeavor looking to his acceptance of positions of public trust or preferment.

Alphonse J. B. Mouthuy.

At his factory on Nichols street, where he has been located since 1801, Alphonse J. B. Mouthuy turns out the highest quality of morocco and fancy leathers generally. His trade is an extensive one, reaching at the present time to such remote parts as France, Germany, and Russia, and giving employment to a large force of men. At the exhibit of the Essex Institute and the Peabody Academy of Science at the World's Fair at Chicago in 1893, specimens of Mr. Mouthuy's products were shown. They received marked attention and were awarded a diploma, by reason of the maker's "skill as an inventor and expert artisan." Mr. Mouthuy was born in Belgium and has been engaged in tanning during his entire business career, his father being of the same craft. He received his education in the Brussels public schools and at the University of Brussels, making a study of chemistry and becoming expert in this branch. No small amount of Mr. Mouthuy's success may be attributed to his wife Emerence, who assumes entire charge of the finishing department at the Nichols street factory. Since his residence in this country Mr. Mouthuy has taken an active interest in politics as a republican, but has never held public office.

Angus Macdonald.

Angus Macdonald, proprietor of the tailoring establishment at 202 1-2 Essex street which has so wide a reputation for

ANGUS MACDONALD.

its fine line of work produced, was born at Springton, P. E. L. Dec. 2, 1856. He was educated in the public schools of the neighborhood and subsequently learned the tailoring business in all its details. From March, 1887, to October, 1888, he was employed in Almy, Bigelow & Washburn's custom department, but resigned to accept a position as cutter with a Boston establishment. Mr. Macdonald afterwards returned to Salem and was for some time connected with the business of John C. Macdonald, opening his present store July 1, 1896. By strict attention to the work in hand, first class goods, fine workmanship and reason able prices, Mr. Macdonald has secured a fine patronage. He is known for his many obliging qualities and as a result has a host of friends. He is an active Mason, a member of Winslow Lewis commandery, Knights Templars, and is chief of Clan Wallace, Order of Scottish Clans.

Salem Cadet Band.

The Salem Cadet band deserves especial notice, not only for the excellence of its music and extensive repertoire, but for its thorough knowledge of the duties of a military band. No details however minute, escape the attention of the leader and it has been aptly termed the band of New England. That it has a

JEAN M. MISSUD.

SALEM CADET BAND

most enviable reputation is evidenced by the large and enthusiastic audiences that gather whenever it plays and by the numerous laudatory home and foreign press notices which are alone sufficient to fill a volume such as this. It has also received the endorsement of the biggest musical authorities. To Jean M. Missud, the talented and popular leader, is due much of the praise for the wonderful proficiency which the band exists it. It was in who, in 1878, organized at ... the second corps of Cadets in ... form as an ... on he has been ... delicate, able in ... the organization, and ... stands w... one of ... the ... wor... [illegible column of text] ...

and his compositions have been most successful. As a leader and organizer, he possesses ability of a superior order and his men are trained, not only musically, but to comport themselves in true military style. They have a national reputation and ...

Joshua Phippen.

JOSHUA PHIPPEN.

[illegible column of text continues around image]

engaged in clerical work with the Salem National bank but determined to make music his profession, with the piano forte as a specialty, although he has had pupils in harmony, counter-point, composition, voice, violin and organ. In 1888 he made a visit to Europe. For many years he has been curator of music at the Essex Institute, where for a number of seasons he managed chamber concerts. Several years ago he gave a series of ten recitals playing largely from memory. His repertory includes practically all of the standard works for the instrument. As a teacher Mr. Phippen has had the good fortune to instruct many talented pupils, several of whom have, in turn, become successful teachers. He was organist at St. James' church, Boston, for eleven years and for two years at the Arlington street church in the same city. On several occasions he has acted as organist for the Apollo and Cecilia clubs of Boston, and for the Salem Oratorio society. He has appeared in concerts and recitals in Boston, New York and other large cities with marked success. He is constantly at work in the way of composition, but has published little and makes no effort to bring the same to a performance. On two occasions he has submitted compositions in competition for prizes and has won both times, the last prize being $200 awarded by Dvorak at the National Conservatory of Music, New York, for the best concerto for piano forte and orchestra. Mr. Phippen married Miss Addie E. Greeley of Winchester and resides in that town.

Edward F. Lovejoy.

But few musicians of Mr. Lovejoy's age have gained such a wide spread reputation as a scientific and successful artist. His ability has its recognition in the increasing responsibilities placed in his charge.

EDWARD F. LOVEJOY.

His training began very early in life as a choir boy under S. B. Whitney of the Church of the Advent, Boston. At the age of sixteen, Mr. Lovejoy began a course of systematic study under the following instructors, whose names alone offer an unquestionable testimonial: Vocal culture, George L. Osgood; opera, Arthur J. Hubbard; oratorio, Myron W. Whitney; harmony, theory and composition, Stephen A. Emery of the New England Conservatory of Music, also Thomas Tapper, examiner of the American College Musicians; piano, J. B. Mason and Joshua Phippen; physiology, hygiene, throat and lung diseases, the late Dr. Hendickson. After five years' study, Mr. Lovejoy made an extensive tour under the management of R. M. Floyd, now president of the Boston Conservatory of Music. The success of this move was most marked and Mr. Lovejoy was prevailed upon to accept a position at the head of the vocal department of the Rockford, Ill., Conservatory of Music. Later, he went to Wesleyan Female college, Macon, Ga., as principal of the vocal department, also holding the chair of professor of physiology and science of vocal art. At both Rockford and Macon, Mr. Lovejoy's labors were crowned with the highest success. The exacting duties and the extreme heat at the south caused a severing of this last relation, with much regret on both sides. Mr Lovejoy now has a studio in this city, his time being devoted to teaching, lecturing upon musical subjects, conducting choirs and choruses and singing in concerts and oratorios. His compositions are of a classical nature, largely church anthems, numbers for male quartets, etc. He has also made successful ventures in the operatic line and has frequent articles in New York journals. He is author of the books, "To Sing or Not to Sing," "Physical Development," "Breathing Exercises," etc. He is extremely popular, commanding the respect and confidence of all who know him. His cheerfulness acts as a magnet to draw out the best efforts of pupils. Mr. Lovejoy realizes that none can succeed in an effort for which he possesses no talent or relish, for while his wide study and experience fit him to become proficient in many things, his tastes have directed him to the particular calling in which he has won an enviable position.

Dr. C. S. Dennis.

The age of miracles may have passed, but in these modern days we are sometimes confronted with entirely inexplicable phenomena. In this class we must place the experiences of Dr. C. S. Dennis and his successful practice as a healer of all kinds of diseases. Of late years much attention has been drawn to magnetic healing, and it is by this name, for want of a better, that Dr. Dennis characterizes his cures, though he can by no means explain the marvellous powers with which he is mysteriously endowed. Dr. Dennis was born in Beverly, April 12, 1853.

DR. C. S. DENNIS.

When a young man he learned the carpenter's trade, and he so occupied himself until seven years ago, when a severe shock of paralysis seized him. Previously he had suffered two minor attacks of the same nature, one when he was eighteen years of age and another ten years later. By the latest and most severe affliction, the victim was incapacitated from work of any kind. At that time he had almost no use of his feet and his articulation was so indistinct that he could be scarcely understood. Sunday evening, November 30, 1890, the afflicted man was sitting at his home with a party of friends, when he felt a rubbing motion, apparently administered by human hands on his limbs, thigh, and side, and afterward upon his throat and head. The family physician, who had been attending the patient during his illness, was present and his astonishment may be imagined when the paralyzed man spoke with a clear and distinct voice which before had been painfully incoherent. Mr. Dennis' first words were in joyful announcement of his cure, and to show that the recovery was not a delusion, he immediately began to run up and down stairs. From that day to this he has had nothing but the best of health. By Spiritualists, the cure has been accounted supernatural, but the doctor is compelled to leave it unexplained though inclined to the belief that the wonderful manifestation was due to some higher natural law not yet fully understood. For several years the subject of our sketch has had peculiar powers, inasmuch as he could under certain conditions, see objects and persons apparently in life, who were dead or far away. The facts of his sudden cure are attested by a large number of credible witnesses. The event caused a great sensation, an extended account appearing in the Associated Press despatches of December 4, 1890, and which was published in leading papers in this country and in Europe. Almost in a day the correspondence of the humble Beverly carpenter reached to enormous proportions and it was impossible to make replies. But the sequel to this event was not less wonderful than the deed itself. Ever since his own cure, Dr. Dennis has been possessed of a wonderful gift in the way of assisting others who may be afflicted in body. Notwithstanding his entire lack of regular medical training, he has cured hundreds of difficult cases, many of which had been given up by regular practitioners. We can name only a few such instances. All these cures were effected largely by the laying on of hands, for the healing power, which the doctor himself cannot explain, seems to lie largely in his hands. Among the most wonderful cures was that of Albion Frye, 51 Front street, Beverly, who was freed from the tortures of inflammation of the spinal blade and sciatic nerve. after having been treated at hospitals by the best doctors in the state with no lasting results. The man was in a most pitiable condition and the facts of his cure spread rapidly. James W. Conlin, a Haverhill boy, was cured after wearing leg and hip irons for five years. He now walks without support and his injuries are healed. William Eastwood of St. John, N. B., now of Centre street, Danvers Centre, was cured of a severe spinal trouble, after having been refused admission at two leading hospitals on account of the reputed hopeless character of his complaint. And so instances might be multiplied. Every case can be vouched for, as they are well known to hundreds, and have been duly sworn to in legal depositions by the grateful patients. Dr. Dennis may be consulted in Salem on Tuesday, Wednesday, Friday and Saturday of each week, at his office, room 5, 81 Washington street. Most nobly is he exemplifying the words, "The best part of the record of every man's life is what he has done for others."

Charles P. Winchester.

Years of experience as an instructor, a thorough and practical knowledge of musical instruments, personal attention to each and every pupil, and a central location, are a few of the reasons why Charles P. Winchester, teacher of the banjo, guitar, and mandolin, with rooms in the Price block, 237 Essex street, has always had the most liberal support in his efforts to furnish the very best instruction upon these favorite instruments. Mr. Winchester was born in Gloucester, February 3, 1866, and has always resided either in that city or Salem. He attended the Gloucester public and high schools, but for the last fifteen years has devoted his entire time to his profession, among his teachers being Luis T. Romero, the famous musician of Boston, now deceased, Frank L. Collins of Boston, instructor in harmony, and Prof. A. A. Babb. Mr. Winchester played the cornet with various bands for seventeen years, but gave this up that he might give undivided time to his stringed instruments, and is now acknowledged to be one of the most finished players in this section, appearing with great success at concerts and other musical events in various cities. At the close of each season, Mr. Winchester's pupils give a public recital, which is one of the musical treats of the year. Mr. Winchester is a member and director of the Arion banjo, mandolin and guitar club

FRANK B. COX.

of this city, of Constantine lodge, K. of P. of Gloucester, and of Gloucester division, Uniformed rank of the same fraternity. He is married, has three children, and resides at 32 Leach street.

Frank B. Cox.

Although but recently established in the real estate and insurance business Mr. Cox has been most successful in building up an excellent clientele. Previous to entering upon his present occupation, he was with the P. A. Davenport Manufacturing company, New York City. Mr. Cox represents some of the best fire insurance companies and also makes a specialty of loans and mortgages. He has devoted much attention to building homes for the working classes and offers every inducement to persons of limited means to acquire their own homes upon the most reasonable terms. Mr. Cox is a native of Roxbury, where he was born in 1869. He was educated in the public schools of Boston and came to reside in Salem in May last.

Lewis B. Moody.

Among the old time business houses of Salem, the establishment of Lewis B. Moody stands pre-eminent and is an example of the success which can be achieved by businesslike methods and strict integrity of purpose. Mr. Moody was born in Salem in 1830, receiving his education at the public schools and when but seventeen years of age engaged in business for himself as a newsdealer and stationer. He has occupied his present store at 151 Washington street since 1861, and has built up an excellent trade which continues to grow with each succeeding year. The lines dealt in include stationery, books, newspapers and periodicals, fancy articles, jewelry, spectacles, cigars and other goods and are all up to date in every essential. The stock is carefully chosen and adapted to the requirements of his patrons, and the store is favorably known to every resident of Salem and its environs. Mr. Moody has never aspired to public office, but has throughout his career devoted his entire attention to the requirements of his business in which he is ably assisted by his son, Lewis C. Moody.

LEWIS B. MOODY.

FOREST RIVER LEAD WORKS.

NEW DRYING ROOM. FOREST RIVER LEAD WORKS.

Forest River Lead Works.

These works were founded and incorporated in 1840 as the Forest River Lead company and were in active and successful operation for more than forty years under this designation. In 1884 they were purchased by the Chadwick Lead works of Boston, and by them remodelled, enlarged and much improved, increasing their capacity very extensively. The name was changed to Forest River Lead works to avoid conflicting with the original company which was still in existence. On the night of March 5, 1897, the entire main factory was destroyed by fire, causing heavy financial loss, aside from the great interference with the extensive business of the company. It was immediately decided to rebuild on still more extensive plans, the result of which is one of the largest, finest and best arranged white lead works in the country, embracing all the new and latest improvements in machinery and appliances, with every facility for manufacturing the highest grade of white lead. They are fully equipped with automatic sprinkler system for the prevention of fire and also with pneumatic watchman's check. Their present capacity is about 6,000 tons per annum and the manufacture is entirely by the "Old Dutch Process," which has been in use for more than 300 years, the product of which far excels in opaqueness, fineness, body and wearing qualities any of the quick process products on the market, and exceeds them in covering qualities to a large extent. That the Forest River white lead has fully stood the test required of a first class product is demonstrated by the great demand for it by the trade and painters throughout New England and other portions of the United States. The Forest River Lead works are situated on Lafayette street at Forest river and are the only works of the kind in this city. Elisha C. Sloan is superintendent. The Chadwick Lead works own and operate a large factory in Boston for the manufacture of lead pipe, sheet lead block tin pipe, tin-lined pipe etc., also extensive oxide works for the manufacture of red lead, litharge, etc., for rubber and glass manufacturers' use and other purposes, at East Cambridge. The officers and managers of the Company are J. H. Chadwick, president, who, with E. D. Ingraham and R. Bampton, Jr., are the directors. The offices are at 176-184 High street (Fort Hill Sq.), Boston, Mass., where all communications should be addressed.

Vaughn Machine Co.

"The practical and economical use of machinery in most of the processes of leather making dates from the inception of the Vaughn ideas in leather working machines." This was the statement made by a leather manufacturer recently, and the rapid change going on in the leather manufactories of the country in the substitution of machine work for hand labor, bears out the statement. Although there have been machines devised doing away with hand labor to a certain extent, only since the Vaughn patents have been on the market has the use of machines in most of the more tedious operations been general. For years the only improvements in methods of preparing hides and skins were those looking to the subdivision of processes. Hand labor continued to be the mainstay of the tanner, currier and morocco manufacturer, and for taking the stretch and bag out of partially processed hides and skins for fleshing. For the proper manipulation in various processes it was thought that, from the complex nature of the operations required, machines would never be able to accomplish the results of hand work. This impression was dissipated by the Vaughn patents and it was shortly demonstrated that not only could equal results of hand labor be secured, but better effects came from machine work than from the most skilled hand labor. As soon as this became demonstrated, it only became a question of manufacturing the machines with sufficient rapidity to meet the demands of manufacturers desirous of securing the improved results and the greater economy made possible by the machines. In filling this universal demand the largest business in the world in its line has been built up. Leather machinery of all kinds to meet all demands whether of heavy or light weight hides and skins, are now made by the concern. Thorough and practical experience in all of the various branches of leather manufacture, a careful study of the different methods and the requirements of different stock have made it possible for the Vaughn Machine company to meet the exact requirements of each customer, and to make their machines an unfailing success wherever they have been placed. About four years ago the company was compelled to seek larger quarters, and they have now a complete and thoroughly equipped plant for the manufacture of their machines from the raw material.

THE VAUGHN PLANT.

The works are situated at Newhall's, a station on the South Reading branch of the western division of the B. & M. R. R. The main building was formerly a print works, and is a substantial brick structure of three stories. To this have been added a series of buildings forming the various accessory work shops and outbuildings, the latest being a commodious foundry, and thoroughly equipped with the latest machines and tools for the brass and iron casting required. Every detail entering into the manufacture of the machines is now performed at the works; and the raw material is received by rail at the factory door. The machine shop runs the whole length of the building and is one of the best equipped in Massachusetts. Here all planing, turning and fitting are done, and an immense lathe of seven foot swing is located, with boring machines and planers, of corresponding capacity; also automatic gear cutting machines, lathes for simultaneous boring and turning and a special lathe for cutting the spiral grooves for blades in the cylinders of the various machines. The motive power is both steam and water, the former of 175 horse power capacity and the latter of forty. They can be used singly or together as desired, and give practically unlimited power. Dynamos furnish light for the entire plant. On the first floor is the setting up shop, where machines are put together. The wood working shops, blacksmith shops and blade works are in new buildings constructed for these purposes. The upper floor of the main building contains the department for the construction of the cylinders which form an important feature of the Vaughn machines. An idea of the construction of these ingenious cylinders may be gained from the illustration. They consist of hubs of metal and iron into which are set blades running in oblique lines, in a complicated pattern, and arranged so that when the cylinder revolves, the leather against which it presses is stretched in both length and width at the same time. The cylinders are channelled on the special machine before referred to and the knives are pressed in by a press exerting an enormous pressure. The offices of the company, convenient and handsomely fitted

GEORGE C. VAUGHN.

IRA VAUGHN.

on all kinds of skins is now accomplished by its use. The beam-house machine, patented in 1887 and since constantly improved, is used for fleshing, unhairing and slating, scudding or finehairing. For three years past, the company has been making a machine similar in construction, but with additional improvements for scouring, stoning-out and setting all kinds of side leather and it is now adopted by leading tanners and curriers. The company has also invented and acquired the following machines, which they manufacture: the Batchelder blacking machine, patented in 1882, and the only device invented for this purpose. It is in use by the largest currying shops for blacking, gumming and pasting wax leather in sides or calfskins, also for staining, blacking and finishing satin, oil and grain leather. The company has been making bark cutting machines since 1891, and has attained perfection in its No. 4 cutter. The Coombs in natural wood, are on the upper floor of the building. The entire plant is so arranged that the work progresses naturally from one department to another, access to the different floors being secured by convenient stairways and an elevator of unusual size. From 150 to 200 employes are on the payroll of the company, all skillful mechanics receiving wages commensurate with their skill. The management is careful of the comfort of the employes and a position with the company is considered desirable by the mechanics of this vicinity. The putting-out machine made by the concern, was invented in 1882, by J. W. Vaughn, father of the present members of the firm. Since then the machine has been constantly improved, each change bringing it nearer to perfection. To-day it has become the standard machine in the morocco and light leather trade, being used exclusively all over the world. Nearly all the striking-out and putting out

CHARLES P. VAUGHN.

BARK CUTTING MACHINE

BATCHELDER BLACKING MACHINE.

BARK CUTTING MACHINE.

BEAM HOUSE MACHINE.

PUTTING-OUT MACHINE.

COOMBS JACK, FOR ROLLING AND GLOSSING

BEAM HOUSE MACHINE

ROOD SHAVING MACHINE

Eight Leading Machines Manufactured by the Vaughn Machine Co.

EXTERIOR VAUGHN MACHINE CO. GERMAN OFFICE, FRANKFORT.

INTERIOR GERMAN OFFICE, VAUGHN MACHINE CO.

FACTORIES, VAUGHN MACHINE CO.

jack for rolling and pebbling leather was invented by Thos. Coombs, now in the employ of the company, in 1890. In 1886, John Rood, while in the employ of the company, invented the Rood Shaving machine by which nearly all leather and skins are now shaved. The company is selling agents for the belt knife splitting machine, manufactured by the American Tool and Machine co. The belt knives made by the Vaughn Machine co. for this machine are the best on the market. A new machine recently invented is for whitening and buffing leather. The new staking machine has larger capacity and requires less power and space to operate than any other, while the iron frame glazing machines are being adopted by the largest morocco firms in the country. By means of the wet stretching machine for belt leather, made for the past two years by this company, belting strips are stretched thoroughly in a wet state. The Cryderman adjustable angle iron and jaw plates for belt knife splitting machines are in universal use. The latest invention of the Vaughn company is a machine having an enormous capacity for unhairing, fleshing and scudding goat, sheep, calf and kangaroo skins, and it has far exceeded the most sanguine expectations. The Vaughn trade extends not only throughout the United States, but to Canada, Mexico, South America, Europe, Australia and New Zealand, and is annually increasing in volume. The company's headquarters and offices in Europe, of which exterior and interior views are shown, are in Frankfurt a Main, Germany, James Sharp, who was formerly a large and well-known leather manufacturer in Chicago, and who entered the employ of the company some two years ago, being in charge. They also maintain an office at 11 High St., Boston, and ware rooms, and a repair shop at 429 Oriana St., Phila.

Essex Credit House.

M. Newmark, proprietor of the Essex Credit House, Essex street, has been engaged in business in Salem for the past fourteen years. Starting in at seventeen years of age to seek his fortune, he may justly be termed a self-made man, achieving success from a small beginning with but energy and brain for capital. As may be inferred from the name of the establishment he conducts, this enterprise is carried on largely upon the credit system, and under his judicious management the trade has developed rapidly, until it now covers an extensive district. Watches, diamonds and jewelry are handled, besides a full and strictly up-to-date line of ladies' and gentlemen's clothing, including garments for the young of both sexes. Any article needed in these various departments may here be obtained by the credit principle, upon the most liberal

M. NEWMARK.

terms and at prices which place this house in the position of an active competitor with the largest concerns in or out of the city. This cannot but prove a boon to persons of moderate or limited means and the proportions to which the trade has grown attest the appreciation of their patrons with regard to the idea. A traveling collector is constantly employed. He is thoroughly public-spirited and is active socially, being affiliated with the Masons, Red Men and A. O. U. W.

Parker Brothers.

From a small beginning has arisen a business which is well-known, not only in our own country, but in many foreign parts of the world. The first of the Parker games was invented by George S. Parker when a boy in the high school. It was called "Banking" and its success was such as to warrant the young publisher in originating and publishing several additional games in the following year. The line was again increased, and in 1886 a store and office were opened in the Franklin building, on the corner of Washington square, under the name of Geo. S. Parker & Co. Lawn tennis was at that time coming into vogue, and was, in addition to the parlor games, sold at wholesale and retail. The business developed rapidly, and in 1888 Charles H. Parker left other business to become a member of the firm. From this time the name of the firm became Parker Brothers, and through the united efforts of the brothers, has grown to its present importance. The Parker games include over 200 varieties, ranging from scientific games such as "Chivalry" to simple and laughable pastimes which have, nevertheless, scored immense successes, such as "Tiddledy Winks" and "Pillow Dex." The list includes educational, literary, humorous and strategetic games and puzzles. The firm occupies the whole of the three story building on the corner of Bridge and St. Peter streets and lease portions of other buildings. A large addition to the present building is now contemplated. Parker Brothers' travelers cover the entire country from Maine to California. The firm also does the largest export business in games of any house in the country, and has agents in England, Canada, Australia and South America. The factory of this concern which has been greatly enlarged within a few years, employs a large number of hands adding much to the prosperity of Salem.

PARKER BROTHERS' FACTORY

Alden P. White.

District Attorney Alden P. White is distinctively an Essex county man. His ancestry reaches through typical and familiar county families; and he cherishes the New England spirit and traditions with loyal enthusiasm. He was born in Danvers in 1850, spending ten years of his childhood in South Danvers, now Peabody, and receiving his early education in the public schools of that town, Danvers and Salem. Mr. White graduated with honors with the Amherst class of '78, and after a course at the Harvard law school, studied at the office of Perry & Endicott, Salem. He was admitted to the Essex bar in 1881 and has been in constant practice ever since, with offices at Salem. In 1890 he was appointed a special justice of the First Essex district court, resigning to accept the position of assistant to Hon. William H. Moody, during the latter's first term as district attorney, and was re-appointed three years later. Upon Mr. Moody's promotion to congress, Mr. White was his logical successor, and in his administration he has fulfilled every expectation created during his earlier connection with the office, taking high rank among the legal men of New England. Outside of his official work, Mr. White has been largely interested in matters of general public concern and has served upon the school committee and as a trustee of the Peabody Institute of Danvers, director of the Essex Institute of Salem, and president of the Salem Oratorio society. He was also one of the founders of the Danvers Historical society. Mr. White is known as one of the ablest members of the Essex County bar and is a hard student of his chosen profession.

Leroy B. Philbrick.

One of the largest dealers in his line and a representative business man of the city is Leroy Batchelder Philbrick, whose store is located at 75 Washington street. He is a native of Hooksett, N. H., and son of the late Almon O. Philbrick, who died when the subject of this sketch was seven years old. Mr. Philbrick remained upon the home farm until the age of fifteen, acquiring a sound constitution and a thorough moral training. Leaving home, he began work in a grocery store at Newburyport, removing from there to Haverhill, where he learned the hat and cap business. Later, he attended the East Greenwich academy and the Providence Conference seminary and secured a most practical education. He was for some time a salesman for a wholesale hat concern in Chicago, coming to Salem in 1867 as a traveling salesman for Stover Grindal, at that time a leader in the business of wrapping paper, bags, twine, etc. In 1872 Mr. Philbrick bought his employer out and formed a partnership with F. W. Perkins, with whom he continued on Central street until 1885, when a removal was made to the present quarters, adding a line of paints, oils, glass

DISTRICT ATTORNEY ALDEN P. WHITE.

and painters' supplies generally. Oct. 1, 1894, upon the decease of his partner, Mr. Philbrick assumed control of the entire business, which is constantly increasing in its volume. Besides the store trade, teams cover Essex county and the city of Lowell, supplying paper bags, twine, etc., to dealers in various lines. A salesman is also engaged in the paint, oil and glass trade in Salem, Danvers, Peabody and Gloucester. Mr. Philbrick has long been active in religious work and has just completed his twenty-fifth consecutive year as superintendent of the Central Baptist Sunday school. For about eight years he has resided on Winter street.

Frank G. Rich.

The youngest man in Salem or vicinity engaged in the confectionery trade is Frank G. Rich, proprietor of the establishment known as the Philadelphia Candy Store, and located at 244 Essex street. Some three and one half years ago he succeeded his father, Snow Rich, in the management of this business, which had been conducted most successfully for the nine years previous by the elder Rich. The present proprietor learned the trade in his father's employ, and was thus brought in contact with the most skilled workmen in the business, as only the best find employment here. Since assuming control, he has increased the scope of the business quite extensively and has made many noticeable improvements about the store. A magnificent steel ceiling has been placed in position and the general interior decoration is most tasty. A fine showcase, eighteen feet in length, is a recent acquisition. Candy is handled exclusively, which makes the store a busy place at all times, particularly during holiday seasons. The wholesale custom, including supplies furnished churches, societies, fairs, etc., reaches large proportions. Specialties are made of Christmas and Easter novelties, fancy chocolate packages and german favors. Mr. Rich is an Odd Fellow and is also connected with the Order of United American Mechanics

LEROY B. PHILBRICK.

and with the Now and Then Association.

William P. Radford.

William P. Radford was born in Salem in 1864 and received his education in the public schools. Nineteen years ago he opened his present commodious store at 163-165 Washington street, and has since been engaged in the business of a

WILLIAM P. RADFORD.

newsdealer, to which he has added books, stationery, fancy articles, cigars and an excellently equipped lunch counter. The premises are well situated to command a first-class trade, being opposite the B. & M. depot, and he does a large and ever increasing business. Ten years ago Mr. Radford joined interests with A. F. Goldsmith, but since June last has conducted the business himself, devoting his close personal attention to it, with the result that a most pleasing patronage has been built up. Liberality and just dealing have always been his characteristics and he enjoys a full measure of popularity in his native city. He is a member of the Masonic order, I. O. O. F., and of the A. O. U. W.

Joseph F. Full.

Within recent years great progress has been made in the customs for the burial of the dead, and the occupation of the funeral director has risen from a mere mechanical trade to the dignity of a profession. The high position and enviable reputation achieved by Joseph F. Full as a funeral director and embalmer in this city and vicinity, are ample evidences of his fitness for the duties that devolve upon him. Mr. Full has at his undertaking rooms, 36 St. Peter street, every facility and convenience for the conducting of his large business. He takes full and complete charge of all arrangements for burial, furnishes casket, carriages and hearse, arranges all details and personally directs the last rites. Mr. Full makes a specialty of embalming and his ideas in this direction are in the advance of the profession. He is a graduate of Clark's School of Embalming, Boston, and he uses a preparation which is absolutely reliable as an embalmer. Mr. Full is a native of Salem, where he was born in 1838, receiving his education in the public schools, upon leaving which he entered the employ of Merritt's Express company, and for thirty years conducted a tonsorial parlor on Washington street. He has been connected with the direction of funerals for the last nineteen years. He was an active member of the Salem Cadets for twenty-nine years, is a member of the Pilgrim Fathers, Salem Charitable Mechanics' association and is a Mason of high standing. Few in their chosen calling are more popular.

JOSEPH F. FULL.

Geo. A. Collins & Co.

The firm of Geo. A. Collins & Co., is widely and favorably known, being one of the largest and most progressive concerns in the jewelry business, and enjoying the extensive patronage of the people of Salem and vicinity. It is interesting to note that enterprise, industry and popularity are qualities bound to make men successful. The truth of this is signally illustrated in the career of this jewelry firm, for foremost among those engaged in their line of business is the concern of Geo. A. Collins & Co., established in 1875. The elegant and attractive premises occupied at 198 Essex street, are well adapted for the display of the large and beautiful stock of diamonds, jewelry, silverware, clocks, novelties, optical goods and bicycles. Special mention is made of the large stock of fine cut glass which includes many new designs carried by no other concern in Essex county. The entire stock they claim to be the most complete in the city. A decided specialty is made of optical goods and they are the leaders in this line. This department is under the charge of Geo. A. Collins, Jr., a graduate of the Spencer Optical Institute of New York. Having made a study of the eye, he is rapidly attaining a name as a specialist in this profession, and an acknowledged authority on prescriptions. Almost everybody carries a watch, and in C. F. Collins the firm has a member who is a thorough workman, understanding the most intricate parts of the mechanism of both American and foreign makes of watches. The repair department being under his supervision, all entrusting work to him can be sure of having it done in a most satisfactory manner.

Sheplee & Etheridge.

There is probably no profession in which a greater delicacy of feeling is necessitated than in that of the funeral director. It is asserted that the above firm is possessed of the necessary requisites to successfully carry on their business. Oliver C. Sheplee, the senior partner, has been in the business for over eighteen years, and his knowledge of it is most practical. In 1896, he formed the present partnership with John B. Etheridge, since notceably extending the business of the firm. Both partners are energetic men, thoroughly acquainted with the duties of their profession, and possess a courteous demeanor. Their rooms located at 64 Washington street, are fully stocked with high grade goods suitable for occasions where bereavement occurs, meeting the requirements of all classes of pat-

ESTABLISHMENT OF SHEPLEE & ETHERIDGE.

rons. They furnish everything requisite for the plainest or most imposing funerals, are prompt in meeting their engagements, and can always be implicitly relied upon in all matters relating to interments. They make a specialty of embalming and possess the necessary natural endowments, as well as the technical knowledge so peculiarly needful in this business. Oliver C Sheplee was born in Calais, Vermont, in 1842, receiving his early education in the public schools, afterwards graduating from the Barre academy. He is a member of the Granite lodge of masons, Knights of Honor, Royal Arcanum, American Order of Fraternal Helpers and of the Veteran Firemen. John B. Etneridge is a native of Rome, N. Y., where he was born in 1867, and was educated at the Rome high school, and subsequently took a course at the Pulaski Business college, entering upon his present occupation ten years ago. He was for nine years, prior to coming to Salem, in full charge of the large undertaking establishment of A. W. Mudge of Rochester, and is a member of the National Association of Embalmers. The firm has a large and constantly increasing clientele, and its members are among Salem's leading citizens and business men.

Frank E. Smith.

The business of this funeral director was established in 1888, and from that beginning he has achieved a well-deserved success. As a thoroughly competent and conscientious man, Mr. Smith promptly secured the favor and patronage of the public, which has been significantly strengthened within the past few years. His office is at 139 Essex street, where a complete line of funeral requisites, caskets, etc. is kept in stock and where Mr. Smith can be consulted by patrons at all times. Special attention is given to the process of embalming and every detail connected with a burial may be safely left in his hands. Mr. Smith is a member of the Masonic order, the A. O. U. W. and the I. O. O. F. In business circles he is highly esteemed for the just methods he pursues and the strict integrity ever marking his career. His native urbanity in conducting the affairs of funerals has ever been of much satisfaction to bereaved families who have employed him.

FRANK E. SMITH.

CLARENCE S. PUTNAM'S STORE.

Clarence S. Putnam.

Clarence S. Putnam who occupies commodious premises in the Pingree block, 273 Essex street, is the only exclusive dealer in sporting and athletic goods in Salem, and that his enterprise in establishing a store of this kind is appreciated, is best proven by the large and increasing number of his patrons. The premises are handsomely fitted up, lighted with large plate glass show windows, and the stock embraces every description of sporting and athletic goods either for the amateur or professional. A line of golf, base and football outfits is carried, guns and ammunition, fishing poles and baskets, dumb bells, developers, hunting knives and bags, boxing gloves, &c., &c. Mr. Putnam also handles the Crescent, Niagara and Lovell Diamond bicycles, and makes a specialty of bicycle repairing, and the supplying of wheelmen's sundries. His repair shop is thoroughly equipped with the most modern tools and appliances, and only competent mechanics are employed on it. Mr. Putnam was born in Danvers, April 11, 1866, and was educated in the public schools of his native town. He came to Salem in 1895, and engaged in the bicycle business at the corner of North and Federal streets, moving to the Pingree block September 1, 1897. Mr. Putnam is a member of the L. A. W.

and is highly esteemed by a large circle of friends in this city on account of his industry and integrity.

Frank S. Haskell.

Among the more recent acquisitions to the business community of Salem may be mentioned Frank S. Haskell, who conducts a real estate, insurance and general commission business at 138 1-2 Essex street. He has already established the nucleus of a most successful business, possessing the requisites for the advancement of his interests, being ambitious and public spirited and conducting his affairs on strictly business principles. He was born at Gloucester in 1858 and received his education in the public schools. Upon leaving school he engaged in the shoe business in Lynn, where he remained until coming to Salem. On Nov. 2, 1897, he formed a partnership with William F.

FRANK S. HASKELL.

Perry, a well-known merchant and resident of Salem, with the view of enlarging his business and increasing its scope. Both members of the firm are popular in business circles.

1638, was a mere dwelling and is now a part of the house occupied by Abner Goodell. Here were confined a large number of persons accused of witchcraft, of whom many suffered death. Here,

OLD SALEM JAIL, ERECTED 1813.

Salem Jail.

Few, if any, institutions are more conspicuous in the history of the country than is the jail located in the City of Salem. The contrast, however, between the place of restraint of the earlier day and the present structure is as great as can be imagined. The first jail, built in also, was made the final deliverance of those who had fallen victims to this superstition, Salem leading the way in letting in the light upon the witchcraft delusion. The older portion of the present jail, located at the corner of St. Peter and Bridge streets, was erected in 1813. In 1885, a thorough remodelling occurred and the structure was enlarged to

PRESENT SALEM JAIL AND HOUSE OF CORRECTION.

its present capacity. It is, however, probable that another enlargement will have to be made in the near future. The fine brick residence of Sheriff Johnson, who also acts as keeper of the jail, is located in close proximity and is surrounded by beautiful and well kept grounds, in keeping with the general atmosphere of neatness and order. The jail has every precaution for safety and has a capacity of 150 prisoners. Those committed here are largely for short terms, many for the offense of drunkenness, although in the past twelve years six have been held on the charge of murder, all of whom, with the exception of one now confined, have been sentenced to state prison for life. The prisoners do all the work, such as cooking, baking, firing the boilers, etc., the female inmates making clothing for both sexes. The jail serves also as a house of correction and in this department some sixty-five prisoners are employed in making heels, which are sold to help meet the expenses. The jail is conducted most economically and, like the others of the county, is under the supervision of the county commissioners. Sheriff Johnson's first assistant is Warren D. Cobb, John J. Howe, who was first assistant under Keeper Hathaway, acting as turnkey. The other officers are: Steward, G. Frank Derby; outside officer, Francis F. Johnson; shop officer, James W. Bryant; night watchman, Israel Leavitt, physician, Charles A. Carlton, M. D. On three Sundays each month Protestant services are held in the chapel from 9 to 10 A. M., in charge of Rev. Charles H. Puffer, the prison chaplain, and one Sunday of each month Rev. Fr. Murphy conducts a service along Roman Catholic lines.

Col. Samuel A. Johnson.

COL. SAMUEL A. JOHNSON, SHERIFF ESSEX CO

The marked popularity of Col. Samuel A. Johnson, sheriff of Essex county, was attested at the latter vote day which he was chosen to his present responsible position at the fall of 1895. For many years he had served as a deputy sheriff, and upon the retirement of Sheriff Herrick, Mr. Johnson was the eligible successor. He was born in Salem, July 31, 1847, and attended the public schools of the city until nine years of age, at that time removing to Wisconsin. He studied with the class of '69 at Beloit college in that state. Shortly after, Mr. Johnson returned to his native city and studied law in the office of Hon.

William D. Northend; he was admitted to the Essex Bar in September, 1871, and was associated with Mr. Northend for about one year. The next three years were spent in Lynn, in practice with ex-Clerk of Courts Peabody. Col. Johnson has travelled quite extensively in this country and in Europe, residing for some time in Colorado in 1869, and again in 1876 for the benefit of his health. He enlisted as a private in the second corps of Cadets, April 22, 1874, and has served in every office in the corps, being chosen to the command upon the resignation of Col. John W. Hart. Although practically a stranger to public functions, Col. Johnson's incumbency of the sheriff's office has been an eminently able one, the many problems constantly arising in connection with his multifarious duties being handled with care and discretion. Col. Johnson also acts as keeper of the jail in this city and resides in the house near the jail on St. Peter street. He has attained high rank in Masonry and Odd Fellowship, and is also a member of Naumkeag tribe of Red Men and John Endicott lodge, A. O. U. W.

EDWARD B. BISHOP,
Chairman Board of County Commissioners

Edward B. Bishop.

Edward B. Bishop is a native of Harpswell, Me., where he was born in 1835, receiving his education in the public schools of Brunswick. He worked on a farm until sixteen years of age, when he became a ship carpenter, and before his twenty-first year had charge of one of the largest shipyards in Bath. Subsequently, he engaged in the grocery business, and in 1858 went to Boston as a house carpenter, removing to Haverhill the following year. In 1860, he went into the building and contracting business, in which he continued until 1875, when he was obliged to relinquish his business on account of ill health, and shortly afterwards was appointed city marshal. He was also a member of the first common council of Haverhill in 1870 and served as an alderman in 1871-2. From 1876 to 1882, Mr. Bishop was engaged in the shoe business, but after the great fire in 1882 he retired from business, and the same year was elected county commissioner, being re-elected for six successive terms. He was elected chairman of the board in 1887, and has served fifteen years in all. In 1880, he was a candidate for the mayoralty of Haverhill, but was defeated, owing to a coalition of the democrats and republicans. Mr. Bishop is a thirty-second degree mason, and a member of the B. P. O. E. and Red Men.

Samuel D. Smith.

Samuel D. Smith has served upon the board of county commissioners since 1893, being elected as a republican. He is a son of Jeremiah F. and Jane (Dodd) Smith, has resided in Marblehead all his life and was born May 22, 1842. He attended the public schools of his native town, upon leaving which he learned the trade of a shoemaker, and subsequently was associated with his father in cabinet making. In 1866 he entered the grocery business as a clerk, so continuing until 1889, when he began upon his own account in the same line and is still engaged in this business with notable success. Mr. Smith has been an overseer of the poor for a number of years, and for many years served as one of the trustees of the Marblehead Savings bank. He is a member of Atlantic lodge of Odd Fellows. While commanding the hearty support of his fellow citizens in his nominations for places of trust, he has never been particularly prominent in politics, although taking a deep interest in public affairs.

JOHN M. DANFORTH, County Commissioner.

manhood Mr. Jenkins engaged in farming until 1861, when he enlisted in the first Massachusetts heavy artillery, in which he served for three years. In January, 1866, he was appointed deputy

SAMUEL D. SMITH, County Commissioner.

John M. Danforth.

John M. Danforth was elected county commissioner in 1892, and is now serving a second term. He was born in Lynnfield in 1840, and educated at the public schools, upon leaving which he engaged in farming. He was treasurer for twelve years and chairman for eleven years of the board of selectmen and assessors of his native town, and in 1891-2 represented the nineteenth Essex district in the legislature as a republican.

E. Kendall Jenkins.

E. Kendall Jenkins, the county treasurer, is a son of Captain Benjamin and Betsey Jenkins, and was born in Andover in 1831, receiving his education in the public schools of that town. In his early

E. KENDALL JENKINS, County Treasurer.

sheriff by Sheriff H. G. Herrick, and in March of the same year was chosen town clerk, treasurer and collector of his native town. Upon being elected county treasurer in 1878, he resigned these offices and devoted his sole attention to the duties of the new office. Mr. Jenkins has been for a number of years a trustee of the public library at Andover, which was erected to perpetuate the memory of the Andover soldiers who fell in the civil war. He was one of the first to advocate the erection of this fund some building and was one of its charter members. Mr. Jenkins is president of the First National bank of Salem, and throughout the entire course of his public career has enjoyed the respect and esteem of all, for his unvarying courtesy and tried integrity.

Col. John W. Hart.

The efficiency of the police force of Salem is a matter of municipal pride, and is very due to the able administration of the city marshal, Colonel John W. H who was appointed to his present position by General H. K. Oliver, February 1877. Colonel Hart is vice-president of Peabody and Salem. He is a carpenter by trade, and worked at the business until he assumed the duties of his present office. In 1857 he joined the Mechanic Light Infantry of Salem in

which he served until 1861, when, in response to President Lincoln's first call for 75,000 men he joined the Army of the Potomac and was present at the Battle of Bull Run, returning to Salem with his company upon expiration of his three months' term of service. On February 18, 1862, he re-enlisted in the First Heavy Artillery and was for two years stationed at Washington. Subsequently, on May 15, 1864, he was ordered to join the Army of the Potomac under General Grant. He was engaged in the battle of Spottsylvania and served with distinction in all the important engagements, returning to Salem upon Lee's surrender in 1865. In May, 1870, he joined the Salem Cadets, rising through the various ranks and soon to

COLONEL JOHN W. HART, CITY MARSHAL.

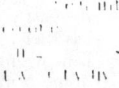

term he was in command of the corps, and is now first lieutenant of Cadets' Veteran corps. He has filled every important office in the G. A. K. and 1878, 1879, he was commander of P. H. Sheridan post. Colonel Hart is prominently associated with the Masonic order, the I. O. O. F., A. O. U. W., and active member of the Essex Institute and of the Young Men's Christian Association of this city.

LELAND H. COLE.

Leland H. Cole.

The portrait of Leland H. Cole will prove a familiar one to all who have business with the Mercantile National bank of Salem, of which institution the subject of this sketch is cashier. He comes of old Salem stock and was educated in the public schools of Beverly. For the past eighteen years he has been identified with banking interests of Salem in the National Exchange and Mercantile banks, assuming his present position in 1894. Although the youngest man in Salem holding a similar office, he is a thorough financier and has proven himself fully competent for the duties devolving upon him. Mr. Cole is a director of the Montserrat syndicate and a trustee of the Kinsman and other large estates, vice president of the Salem Y. M. C. A., treasurer of the Young Men's Republican club, and an Odd Fellow. Adding personal merit to the influence of places of trust, he may well be accorded a prominent place among the highest class of business men in Salem.

Mercantile National Bank.

For over seventy years the Mercantile National Bank has been one of the substantial financial institutions of Salem. Organized May 8, 1826, its entire history has been synonymous with the greatest commercial integrity and its management has always been confided to practical business men of the highest reputation and standing. For decades the Mercantile Bank was located in the building owned by it on Central street, but following the tendency towards centralization of the banking facilities, a removal was made early in 1897 to the Holbrook, No. 228 Essex street. At the

MERCANTILE NATIONAL BANK.

SALEM 1626-1897

new rooms every facility looking to the transaction of the bank's business with safety and despatch is combined with attractive and pleasant surroundings, and during the past four years especially the increase of the business of the bank has been marked. The interior fittings are of solid Mexican mahogany, including a handsomely panelled vestibule at the front door. Heavy plate glass is used liberally and to good advantage on both exterior and interior and the trimmings and railing are of brass and iron. Great care and expense were exerted to secure the best in the way of a vault, which is built double and constructed upon solid masonry, capped with railroad iron, and enclosed with iron and brick work. The vault is designed to be safe from the ravages of fire, and is absolutely burglar proof. Just beyond the business section of the banking rooms are compartments for the use of depositors and leasers of safe deposit boxes. To the rear of this is the directors' room, commodious and handsomely fitted. The ceiling is of stamped steel, decorated in a rose color, and both gas and electricity are used for lighting. The policy of the bank has always been conservative, but withal marked with rare judgment, carrying it safely through the financial flurries and storms of nearly three quarters of a century. The capital at the present time is $200,000, $100 being the par value of the shares. The surplus and profits show a total of $58,000, with deposits of $300,000. The loans and discounts aggregate $450,000, and the total resources are no less than $700,000. The present management is such as to command the confidence of every person doing business with the bank, the directorate including leading financial men of the city. The full list of officers follows: President, William L. Hyde; vice president, David Moore; directors, William L. Hyde, David Moore, John M. Anderson, Matthew Robson, Charles H. Fifield, Walter K. Bigelow, John M. Raymond, George F. Ropes. After the retirement in 1893 of Joseph H. Phippen, whose notable career in connection with the bank is referred to at length elsewhere, Leland H. Cole became cashier, which position he still holds, with Benjamin F. Nason, Alfred Newhall and Walter S. Washburn as teller, bookkeeper and clerk respectively.

Other Banks.

Besides the Mercantile National Bank, conducted under a commendably liberal and independent management, Salem is fortunate in the possession of the following financial institutions: Naumkeag, First, Asiatic, National Exchange, Salem and Merchants' national banks, Salem and Salem Five Cents savings banks, and the Salem and Roger Conant Co-operative banks.

John H. Bickford.

John H. Bickford has achieved an enviable reputation as a consulting electrical engineer, and is a native of Alton, N. H., where he was born in 1860. Coming to Salem at an early age, he attended the public schools. He later studied electrical engineering for which he possessed a natural aptitude and finally secured a position as inspector of the Salem division of the Boston and Northern Telephone company. His skill in his profession speedily became apparent, and he was afterwards offered and accepted the position of constructing engineer for the Sprague Electric Railway and Motor company, New York, which position he acceptably filled for three years, spending some time in the south and west. Subsequently he accepted the position of chief engineer of the Naumkeag Street Railway. Six years ago he opened his present office in the Naumkeag building. Among the most important works designed and constructed by Mr. Bickford may be mentioned the Lynn and Boston street railway plant, the entire plant of the Scranton (Pa.) Traction company, the Reading (Pa.) and Manchester (N. H.) street railway plants. Mr. Bickford also designed and carried out the plans of the very extensive plant of the New York and Queens County railway company, covering the entire area of Queens county and erected at a cost of over $3,000,000. The lighting plant of the Electric Illuminating and Power company of Long Island City and many other works of equal importance were carried out by him. Within the past six months he has added to his regular business an architectural branch and has associated with him H. P. Graves, a very clever and most promising young architect. Mr. Bickford also maintains an office at 20 Broadway, New York.

Charles E. Symonds.

The senior member of the common council in 1807, Charles E. Symonds of Ward 6, has resided in Salem, with slight interruptions in early days since his birth, June 12, 1810. He left the high school when fourteen years of age to engage in boot and shoe manufacturing, continuing in that line for over twenty years, and later entering the probate office as clerk. He was a councilman from Ward 4 in 1854, and in the following year was chosen to the board of principal assessors, resigning after five years' service to accept the office of city treasurer and collector of taxes. In 1865 he resigned to become treasurer and manager of the Salem Savings bank, holding this position until his resignation fifteen years later. Since that time he has been engaged in caring for his own property interests. Besides the two terms in the council already noted, he was a member of that body in 1892 and 1896. He has also been a school committeeman and a member of the board of overseers of the poor. He is thought to be the eldest of a numerous family of that name in Salem and can trace direct connection with Samuel Symonds of Ipswich, who was at one time acting governor of Massachusetts. Mr. Symonds was born in the family mansion at the head of Boston street, close by the Pickering school, and has resided in the house on the corner of North and Dearborn streets for the last forty years.

F. B. Broadhead & Son.

Among the many large insurance firms in the city of Salem, none have better advantages for writing insurance policies than the above concern. Fred W. Broad

JOHN H. BICKFORD.

CHARLES E. SYMONDS.

F. W. BROADHEAD.

head, who is now conducting business under the firm name of F. B. Broadhead & Son, has the distinction of being the youngest man in his line in this section, but his lack of years does not imply any corresponding want in the thoroughness of his commercial training or ability. The foundation of this enterprise was laid ten years ago by the late Frederick B. Broadhead and in 1893 his son, Fred W., was admitted to the firm, assuming full control upon the death of the senior member, Nov. 1, 1896. Through this office, several of the greatest insurance companies in the world are represented, and risks to any amount can be written. Mr. Broadhead has the agency for the Union Mutual Life Insurance company of Maine, incorporated in 1848, which has the reputation of being one of the most reliable and conservative concerns of this character in the world. In the fire line, risks are placed in the following well-known and powerful companies: Agricultural, of Watertown, incorporated in 1851; Hamburg Bremen, of Hamburg, Germany, incorporated in 1854; Manhattan, of New York, incorporated in 1869; Thuringa, of Germany, incorporated in 1853; Standish Life and Accident Co. of Detroit, incorporated in 1874; and United States, of New York, incorporated in 1824. Mr. Broadhead also devotes some attention to real estate matters. His office is most conveniently located on Essex street, near Washington street, and there is every facility for the transaction of a large amount of the best class of business. He has proven himself amply able to sustain the high reputation which became associated with the business in its earlier days, even increasing the same as its scope becomes enlarged.

John B. Harding.

Few men are better known in Salem than the subject of this sketch, John B. Harding, the veteran horse shoer. It will be a surprise to many of Mr. Hard-

JOHN B. HARDING.

ing's friends to learn that he was not born in this city, but in the town of Benedicta, Me., a small hamlet in the heart of the great wilderness of Aroostook county, where his father lived for a few years. The late David Harding, father of John, was shoeing horses in Salem seventy or eighty years ago. At that time he did shoeing for the old Eastern Stage company, which, long before the advent of steam railroads, operated a line of stage coaches between Boston, Portsmouth and Portland. This early smithy was located in what is still known by old residents as the "West Yard," now in the rear of Almy, Bigelow & Washburn's store. There are few, if any, now living who can remember when the fires were first lighted on David Harding's forge. Upon his return to Salem, the elder Harding, after working a while for James Clark, to whom he had sold his business, finally repurchased it. John was taught the family trade by his father at an early age, and for more than thirty years he has been constantly engaged at the anvil. No one in Salem understands better how to make and fit a shoe, and, as he gives the business his constant personal attention, the horse-owners of Salem and vicinity make no mistake in according him a liberal patronage. About four years ago improvements made by Almy, Bigelow & Washburn necessitated a removal from the old historic stand in the "West Yard," and Mr. Harding now has ample quarters and an increasing business at 13 Brown street.

W. H. H. Palmer.

W. H. H. PALMER.

One of the most important features of the trade accommodations of Salem is the clothing and furnishing house of W. H. H. Palmer, which was established by W. H. Palmer, father of the present proprietor, in 1845. The sales rooms are located at 238-240 Essex street and are ample for the large trade carried on. Mr. Palmer carries a large and varied stock, selected with much care to meet the requirements of a critical patronage. The assortment includes full and complete lines of fine and medium clothing for old and young men, all being superior in quality, design, style and fit, fully equal in every respect to custom made garments with the further advantage of being much less in price. This house was the first to introduce the one-price system in Salem and the success they have achieved is most pronounced. Everything in the way of men's furnishings is dealt in, fine white and negligee shirts, underwear, collars and cuffs, umbrellas and all the numerous articles of dress which go to complete a gentleman's attire. A specialty is made of mackintoshes and water-proof goods, bicycle and golf suits and hose, cardigan jackets, sweaters, etc. Mr. Palmer succeeded his father in the business which he has conducted for the past fifteen years in a manner that reflects the utmost credit upon his executive ability and integrity. The trade of this concern extends generally throughout Essex County and dences and factories in that town, Salem, Danvers, Great Falls, N. H., and elsewhere. He afterwards gave his whole attention to designing; and besides his large amount of work in this city, has planned handsome residences in Topsfield, Beverly, Lynn, South Braintree and other places. He designed the extensive remodelling at the summer residence of Endicott Peabody and also rebuilt his large and extensive stock farm buildings, and designed buildings at the farm of Hon. William C. Endicott." The Manning block, a cut of which accompanies

NEW MANNING BLOCK, E. B. BALCOMB, ARCHITECT.

Mr. Palmer enjoys an excellent reputation in the business community.

Edwin Burnham Balcomb

Was born in Yarmouth, Nova Scotia, coming to Salem with his parents at the age of fourteen. He completed his education in the private schools and learned the trade of a carpenter and joiner. Later, he attended drawing school and studied architecture with Robert Bruce. Soon after his marriage Mr. Balcomb began business for himself in carpentry and architecture at Peabody, constructing resi- this article, was built from his plans, as have been a large portion of the newer school houses in Hamilton and Danvers, and engine houses of Peabody. Mr. Balcomb has made a special study of heating and ventilating methods. This, added to his practical knowledge of carpentry and its allied branches, gives him an obvious advantage over those of his profession who lack this experience.

C. H. & J. Price.

The drug business conducted under the firm style of C. H. & J. Price at 226 Essex street, Salem, is the largest of its kind in Essex county, as has been the case for the last half century. The enterprise was founded by Benjamin F. Browne in 1826. The senior partner in the firm of the present day, Charles H. Price, entered the store as a boy, in 1844, but so rapid was his advancement in learning the business that six years later he was admitted to an interest. His brother Joseph, became a partner in 1850, at which time Mr. Browne retired from active business. The third member of the firm is Samuel J. Foster, who was educated in the business by his present partners, assuming an interest after ten years as boy, clerk and in Boston and New York, as well as Salem, but was practically destroyed by the high tariff recently placed upon imported articles. The business has always been located at the present site, the block in which it is located taking its name from the founder. Following a destructive fire in 1861, the store was remodeled, and since that time many great improvements have been made, until it is a marvel of completeness and range. Besides the three proprietors, fifteen clerks are given constant employment. In addition to the immense area of the street floor, five rooms and an attic, besides a large basement, are needed to accommodate the great stock kept on

INTERIOR DRUG STORE OF C. H. & J. PRICE

foreman. A large wholesale as well as retail trade is carried on in that branch of the business, so most important one, many of the sail of stores in Salem and vicinity being supplied with goods from the Price stores. In the former days, when the shipping of this port was Salem's pride and strength, an important feature was the fitting of vessels, and large and dealing with medicine chests. An immense business was also done in the importation of Manila cigars. In one single year the importation exceeded 900,000 cigars. Just got in porting trade success was attained hand. In the basement are large rooms for the manufacturing lines of the stock. Here may be seen the storeroom full of drugs in boxes, the toilet goods, patent medicines, etc., with the preparations of the various houses. A large room for paints and oils, where the heavy stock in use was the general stock of tobacco and supplies have secured a great deal. A new department, however, was the fitting up of a photographic department of great extensiveness on the third floor. George N. Spinney, a gentleman, one of the oldest photographers of the county, has large here. As formerly, cameras, lenses and supplies are kept on hand in large quantities. In addition, amateurs are aided in developing plates, making prints, mounting, etc. A fine dark room has been arranged, which may be used by patrons, when so desired, in the bringing out of work taken in hand. Charles H. Price is one of the leading business men of the city of Salem, having extensive interests in addition to those upon which this article treats. He is president and one of the directors of the Holyoke Mutual Fire Insurance company, holding similar relations with the Salem Electric Lighting company. In former years he has been active in many other concerns, but now finds his energies sufficiently engaged in connection with those here named. He is prominent in the work of the First Baptist church and has served as treasurer since 1846. The same diligent attention and successful results which have marked his efforts in his own behalf have been brought to bear in his administration as the head of these large enterprises of a semi-public nature. Returning to the Price business, it may truly be said to constitute a landmark in this city of ancient and historic spots. For several decades the sign, "C. H. & J. Price," has hung over the Essex street entrance, and the inscription has become a household word in practically every home in the country hereabout. The generation now grown remember it from youth's days. To say that a firm of this standing and continuity had come into the confidence and respect of the people would be absurdly superfluous. It is bringing to itself fine talent in the younger men who are now associated with it, and for many years to come will, beyond a doubt, remain a leading figure in the commercial life of this city. In this well patronized store is combined the up-to-date retail establishment of unquestioned reliability and the large wholesale business equal to that of wholesale concerns in even much larger cities than Salem. In all Boston not such a store exists for diversity of the lines carried. Salem is fortunate in having such an establishment on its greatest thoroughfare in a location making it easy of access to both those who live in and out of town.

A ROOM IN C. H. & J. PRICE'S NEW PHOTOGRAPHIC DEPT.

Lynch Bros.

This firm, whose factory is located on Skerry street, manufactures dull and bright dongola kid and black and colored goat and morocco, and also deals in sheepskins and patent leather. The foundation of this enterprise was laid in 1873 by Patrick Lynch, who began business in Beverly at that time, as a member of the firm of Lynch & Welch. The present concern was formed in 1886, David S. and William A. Lynch, brothers of the senior member, being admitted to an interest. The plant covers 60,000 squares feet of land and was formerly known as the Nevins bagging mill. Twenty-five hands are employed, a large part of whom have been with the firm for many years, and the concern is one of the few in the leather industry which continues operations through the year. The capacity is 2500 dozen skins per week and the entire product meets with a ready sale at the factory. Among recent improvements which add largely to the facilities of the plant are the construction of a new brick dye-house and boiler house and a large boiler and engine. The members of this firm are among the best known leather men in the country and have reached their present position by native shrewdness, economy, energy and uprightness.

J. N. & V. S. Peterson.

The above firm are thoroughly up to date contractors and builders, many handsome and substantial structures erected by them standing as monuments to the skill and thoroughness of their constructors. The senior member of the firm is one of Salem's best known men and has been engaged in his present business for many years. Previous to founding a partnership with his younger brother, he was a member of the firm of Hamilton, Balcomb & Peterson. Since severing his connection with that large building concern and associating with Vincent S. Peterson, he has added to his already high reputation as a practical contractor, and the firm has done its full share of the work of constructing the various buildings erected in this city and vicinity. Among the notable buildings put up by Mr. Peterson and his associates should be mentioned the Peabody building, new state Normal school, County court house,

FACTORY OF LYNCH BROS.

J. N. PETERSON.

and most costly buildings in Essex county. The members of this firm are natives of Salem. They are men of sterling business qualifications, conscientious in their operations, whose ability has placed them in the front ranks of concerns in the state in their line. J. N. Peterson was elected a member of the Common Council in 1886 and in 1888. The offices of the firm are in the Price building and the yard and workshops are on North street.

William Penn Hussey.

The name of William Penn Hussey has become a familiar one, even to the people of distant Cape Breton and those in European financial circles. The inhabitants of Cape Breton

Naumkeag building, Peabody town hall, portions of the Salem jail, Post office building, Endicott building, Dickson memorial chapel, Phillips school house, residence of Mrs. A. M. Wheatland, Conrad building, B. W. Currier building, Lynn, and the remodelling of Almy, Bigelow and Washburn's store and the Salem National bank. While some of these edifices were erected while the senior member of this firm was a member of the firm of Hamilton, Balcomb and Peterson, in every case he was closely identified with and personally superintended the work. The firm are now putting up the new Y. M. C. A. building which when completed will be one of the handsomest

V. S. PETERSON.

have cor
rectly come
to consider it
as a potent
one in the
commercial
affairs of that
section, is at
Boston. Com-
paratively ex-
tensive
ments.
ests
Boston Coa
Co. Mr.
C
w
p
Hussey w
the
and is its
general man-
ager
treasurer. He
makes his
home
Danvers
to the
zens
and
d

WILLIAM PENN HUSSEY.

RESIDENCE OF WILLIAM PENN HUSSEY, DANVERSPORT

AN INTERIOR VIEW AT THE PEABODY ACADEMY OF SCIENCE.

went to the state of Kansas, remaining there for quite a time. He brought to his present position unusual talent for the work in hand and expert authorities predict a rosy future for the Broad Cove company, the product being of a very superior quality for domestic consumption and for generating steam. A notable event in the history of the section in which the mines are located was the running of the first locomotive over the railroad recently built to the mines. A facetious newspaper man, writing from that place, is responsible for the assertion that to the inhabitants there, the reputation of even the wise Solomon is eclipsed by the wonder-working name of William Penn Hussey. Ample capital is at command for the carrying out of every needful detail of the business, which is constantly extending in its scope. The Boston office is at 70 Kilby street. Mr. Hussey married the only daughter of W. H. Munro, the millionaire of Martha's Vineyard, and has one son, J. Fred, who assists his father to a large extent in the management of his business affairs. Mr. Hussey is of most commanding physique and has travelled over all the world. He has had charge of the construction of many large public works, including the Boston sewerage system. His home at Danvers is a palatial one and here he entertains quite extensively. He is known there as the honest coal dealer.

Cawley & Trow.

Among the many characteristics which destiny seems to have had in store for the city of Salem, that of becoming a centre for building, contracting and fitting seems to be prominent. Salem's artisans and storekeepers have at easy command ample facilities for the construction in every detail and the most complete furnishing of every variety of residential or business place. In all departments of this immense field nothing ranks higher in importance than the matter of a practical, substantial and safe system of plumbing. Among the several large concerns of this kind which have headquarters here, that of Cawley & Trow is among the foremost. A branch is maintained in the town of Marblehead, at which point the members of the firm give personal attention to all business in hand, which reaches to extensive and constantly growing proportions. The Salem location is at 8 and 10 Central street, convenient to business and residential districts. Here two floors are occupied, with a most spacious workshop in the basement. Plumbing, using that term in its most comprehensive sense, is done in all its branches. The fundamental idea upon which all work is undertaken is that of thoroughness of results rather than a seeming saving in the matter of prices. The firm represents several exceptionally fine systems for the heating of buildings, and contracts in this line, for either hot water or steam, can be undertaken to any extent. No piece of work is so large and none so small but that bona fide estimates can be furnished. A feature of Cawley & Trow's business has been that of testing plumbing work and of making full corrections, when such may be found necessary. Some twenty hands are employed in busy seasons and two teams are in constant use. Henry M. Cawley, senior member of the firm, is a native of New Hampshire, and has travelled quite extensively. He is a member of the Ancient Order of United Workmen and other organizations. James H. Trow is a Danvers boy, learning his trade in Salem, and has been associated with his present partner for the past six years. He is now taking an advanced course in scientific heating and ventilation. The general repute of the firm is most desirable.

H. A. Brooks.

The bindery at which the finishing touches are placed upon this volume is the largest establishment of its kind in Essex county. H. A. Brooks is the proprietor and the location is in the Hale block, Essex street. Mr. Brooks' entire business life has been spent in this city, having learned his trade with Stephen B. Ives, the pioneer book binder of Salem. He is a veteran of the late war, enlisting at first in Co. A of the Fiftieth Massachusetts infantry and he saw one year's active service at this time. He then returned home and worked at his trade for six months. Again enlisting, this time in the frontier cavalry, he served until the close of hostilities. Upon his return to Salem in 1866, he entered the employ of Mr. Ives, acting as manager of the latter's bindery for two years. Mr. Brooks' next connection was with the Salem Press, where he had charge of the binding department for some time. His first venture upon his own account was made in Maynes' block, Essex street, removing later to Browne's block, over Price's store. One room was sufficient at first for the entire business, but increasing patronage demanded more area, until the whole floor was engaged. The present quarters have been occupied about one year, two entire floors being necessary. Orders for stamping, ruling, folding, etc., are promptly filled and a large business is done in the manufacture of blank and the various kinds of commercial books. In busy seasons, fifteen hands are employed. Mr. Brooks is active in the Grand Army and has served as commander of Phil Sheridan Post 34, of this city. He is also a past master workman of Puritan Lodge, Ancient Order United Workman, and is a member of Fraternity lodge of Odd Fellows. He is well known, therefore, in secret orders.

H. A. BROOKS.

INTERIOR BROOKS'S BOOK BINDERY.

W. H. Crosby.

As an undertaker and funeral director, W. H. Crosby of Danvers has succeeded to a business which was established more than a half century ago. He is the only one of his line in the town and has an extensive employment, fully one half of which comes from outside places. The stock of funeral necessities and the general equipment for the conducting of obsequies is complete in every respect. Everything required, including carriages, can be furnished by him. He is a young

he has since conducted with increasing success. He takes a sincere interest in the town's welfare and is connected with the Masons and Odd Fellows. His establishment is at 8 High street, Danvers square.

H. H. Pillsbury.

An energetic and progressive man of Danvers is H. H. Pillsbury, proprietor of the Danvers carriage exchange and livery stables. He is not only a carriage manufacturer, whose light carriages have

W. H. CROSBY.

H. H. PILLSBURY.

and energetic business man and has shown himself to be unusually well adapted to a thorough understanding of the delicacies of the work in hand. He has made a careful study of the embalming art and has at his command every means looking towards the most effective and successful work of this character. He was born in Yarmouth, N. S., and was educated in the schools of that place. In 1891 he entered the employ of George A. Waite of Danvers and readily grasped every detail. Sept. 1, 1895, he purchased the business and good will, which

won him a reputation second to none, but does and makes a specialty of order work and repairing of carriages and harness, as well as buying, selling and exchanging both carriages and horses. He is located in Danvers square, where is his factory and salesroom for harness, robes, whips, blankets and horse furnishings. A large livery stable is connected, also conducted by Mr. Pillsbury. Opposite, at the old historic Berry Tavern is another stable which he carries on. Mr. Pillsbury was born in Newburyport and was educated in West Amesbury, now Merrimac. There he engaged in carriage making in 1868, making vehicles fully up to the high standard set and ever since adhered to by Merrimac manufacturers. Five years later he came to Danvers and engaged in the same business, in which he has made a marked success. His first location was on the Andrew Putnam property on Putnam street. Several years ago he purchased the old Putnam shoe shop and converted the same into his present establishment, raising the front building one story. Besides making excellent workshops for the different branches of carriage work and salesrooms, there is a commodious hall used for balls and social gatherings. Mr. Pillsbury owns and operates a farm of several acres at Danvers Centre, and besides being an expert judge of horses is also a connoisseur of hens, and does a large business in raising poultry and cattle. He is a veteran of the late war, a past commander of Post 90, G. A. R., a member of the Independent Order Odd Fellows and Free and Accepted Masons.

H. F. OLIVER'S PICTURE FRAME FACTORY.

H. F. Oliver.

H. F. Oliver, manufacturer of picture frames, with place of business at 63 North street, was born in Wakefield, in 1851. He learned the trade of a shoemaker, and gained a thorough mastery of all the details of that business. He made shoes for a number of years, and at one time in the state of New Hampshire carried on a manufacturing business on his own account. In 1876 he went to Hartford, Conn., where he learned the picture frame business. He entered into his new occupation with such zest that he soon gained a thoroughness equal to that displayed in making shoes, and he afterwards engaged in the framing business at Nashua and Manchester, N. H. He finally went to Boston, and, with a partner, F. P. Baker,

H. F. OLIVER.

started the manufacture of picture and room mouldings, under the firm name of Baker & Oliver. He then sold out to Mr. Baker, and erected the so called "Blue Building" on Bridge street, where he carried on the same business until about three years ago, when he erected the three story frame structure which he now occupies at 63 North street. Here he does a

since September, 1897, the building being completed at that time. He was born and brought up in this city and began his business career selling the News. He has been engaged in the provision line for himself and for others for the past fifteen years and has acquired a most complete knowledge of every phase of the trade. Six years ago, he became a member of the

STORE D. G. WHELTON

business of framing pictures and making mirrors to order. By far the largest assortment and variety of fine mouldings to be found in Salem is always kept in stock at this establishment. All work is executed reasonably, durably, and in the best of taste.

David G. Whelton.

Mr. D. G. Whelton is proprietor of what is, beyond doubt, the finest market Salem or vicinity. He has occupied his present store at the corner of Essex and North streets

firm of Power & Whelton, whose establishment was located on North street. Upon the dissolution of this partnership, Mr. Whelton engaged his present stand. His trade is of the most desirable character, including as it does the best families of the city. Eleven clerks are employed

INTERIOR D. G. WHELTON'S MARKET.

A handsome design, the soft busy air in the work of delivery. One of the largest cold blast refrigerators to be found anywhere is at hand for the storage of perishable commodities, and a first class trade is now enjoyed by Mr. Whelton.

BUILDING MOVED BY WM. G. EDWARDS.

William G. Edwards.

The largest building moving concern in the county is undoubtedly that of William G. Edwards, with office at 64 Bridge street. The business was founded by J. B. Edwards, father of the present proprietor, some thirty years ago. Gradually and steadily the field has broadened, until at the present time employment is given to a large force of men at all seasons of the year when it is possible to do work of this kind. The apparatus on hand is of the most complete and powerful description. Otherwise such contracts as the removal of the immense brick chimney at the Devlin factory could not be undertaken. This latter work was done in the summer of 1896, the chimney first being removed from its foundation, a new foundation built, upon which the chimney was again placed after having been raised ten feet, and all this done without the semblance of damage or accident of any kind. In November, 1896, the stone and wood residence of William D. Sohier at Beverly, of which a cut is here given, was moved some seventy-five feet to a more sightly location, the several chimneys, fire-places and stone constructions being injured in not the slightest degree. By Mr. Edwards, the removal of stone or brick buildings has been brought to an absolute science. A thorough mechanic himself, he has the confidence of the contractors of the city and is a member of the Master Builders' Association. Estimates of moving, including the raising of roofs, placing in position heavy machinery, etc., will be furnished on application.

H. M. Sinclair.

Should one walk down Washington street past the old stone station, the first thing attracting the attention is the fine assortment of suitings and trouserings displayed in the show window of the custom clothing establishment, of which H. M. Sinclair is proprietor. If one has a few minutes to spare, it may be an advantage to step in and examine the extensive line of samples which are always on exhibition. Having been engaged in the ready-made trade for over

H. M. SINCLAIR.

twenty eight years, Mr. Sinclair is well versed in everything that pertains to the business. Not being entirely satisfied with garments cut on the one pattern plan, giving only to the few the styles and fit that stamp the up-to-date industrial, he decided to start a custom clothing business on his own plan, thereby giving to his patrons the opportunity to purchase a stylish, well made custom garment at prices slightly in advance of those charged for ready made goods. With this end in view, a room was leased in the Hawthorne building and an agency secured from one of the largest New York firms. Here, by strict attention to business and a careful consideration of the wishes of his customers, he has built up for himself a trade that is not excelled by any tailor in the city. Although away from the main street in a quiet, modest way the establishment has forced itself upon the people and today numbers among its patrons many of the most influential citizens of the community. Mr. Sinclair having access to all the leading styles as fast as they appear, and having the largest line of cloths of both foreign and domestic make in New York from which to select, his stock cannot fail to please the public and he is daily adding to the list of his customers. Should one need any suggestions pertaining to the mode of dressing, they will be cheerfully imparted by the genial proprietor of the custom clothing house at 205 Washington street, Salem, Mass.

Thomas Gorman.

Thomas Gorman, who has an office at 2 and 4 Charter street, does a general business in the way of raising and moving

BUILDING MOVED BY THOS. GORMAN.

ARTHUR F. GOLDSMITH.

buildings. Mr. Gorman has resided in Salem for many years and learned the trade of a carpenter. Since 1880, however, he has devoted the larger part of his time to building moving, although occasionally taking carpentering work.

Arthur F. Goldsmith.

Arthur F. Goldsmith was born in Salem and has resided here all his life. In 1868 he began selling newspapers, and two years later was employed by Irving, Stone & Co. where his natural aptitude to learn and the marked ability he displayed in business matters speedily won him promotion. Subsequently he engaged in business for himself, and has gradually worked his way into the front rank of the news-dealers of Salem. At present he employs over one hundred boys, fifty-eight of whom have regular routes, the remainder being used for street sales. Mr. Goldsmith's distributing bureau is at 10 Norman street, and he has agents in every ward of the city. The business has grown to large proportions under his capable management, and a perfect system of organization prevails. All the leading New York, Boston and other newspapers are handled and delivery made at residences throughout the city. Orders from subscribers receive immediate attention. Mr. Goldsmith is well known and much esteemed in business circles and enjoys the respect of his fellow citizens.

John J. Hartigan.

John J. Hartigan, who has a blacksmithing and horse shoeing establishment at 184 Bridge street, learned his trade with his father, Patrick Hartigan, who, in his active business days, was one of the best known

JOHN J. HARTIGAN.

men of his vocation in this vicinity. The younger Hartigan was born in this city in 1852 and has spent his entire life here, graduating from the Phillips school. He was associated with his father from the conclusion of his school days until 1886, when he began business upon his own account. In 1878-9-80-1-2 he was a member of the common council from Ward 1, serving upon many important committees, and in 1892-3 was a candidate from his district for the legislature, and although the district was overwhelmingly adverse politically, he was defeated by but a narrow margin. Mr. Hartigan is an ex-president of the Young Men's Catholic Temperance society, ex-chief ranger of Essex Court of Forresters and past grand knight of Veragua Council, Knights of Columbus. He is also a prominent Elk, member of John Bertram Lodge, A. O. U. W., and has served as president of the Sheridan club.

Salem Carriage Works.

SPECIAL ATTENTION GIVEN TO

REPAIRING, PAINTING AND TRIMMING

OF FINE CARRIAGES.

Orders Taken For Rubber Tires.
Work Called For.

411 Bridge St., Salem, Mass.

Chadwick Lead Works
FOREST RIVER LEAD CO. SALEM Warranted PURE BOSTON CHADWICK LEAD WORKS
176-184 HIGH STREET, FORT HILL SQUARE, Boston
LEAD MERCHANTS AND MANUFACTURERS
Lead Pipe & Sheet Lead. Tin Pipe. Sheet Tin.
RIBBON & TAPE LEAD LEAD SASH WEIGHTS COPPER & IRON PUMPS
TIN LINED PIPE SOLDER BABBITT METAL GLAZIERS METAL
White Lead Dry and in Oil. Red Lead. Litharge. Etc.
Sole Owners of Forest River White Lead Works. Salem, Mass.
ELECTRIC CABLES OF ALL SIZES COVERED WITH LEAD.

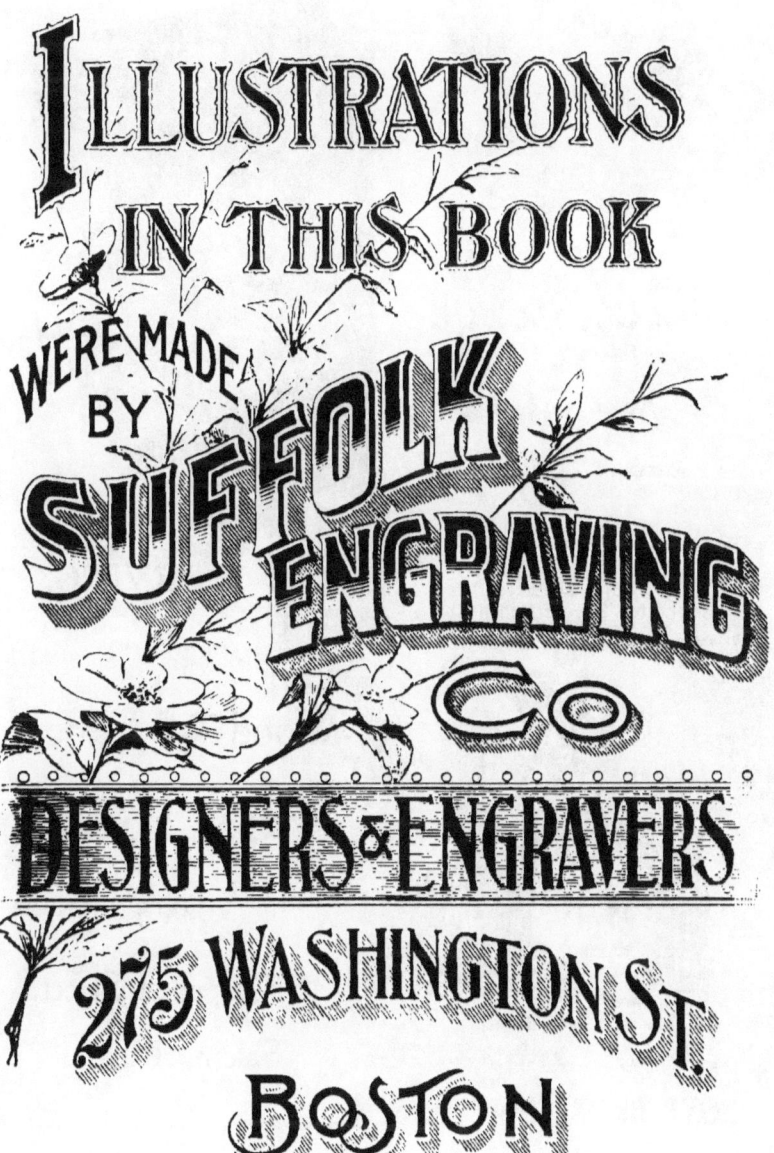

Davis

*Exclusive
and Original Styles
... IN ...
Millinery.*

189 Washington St.,
Salem, Mass.

The CHEF OF DELMONICO'S could not prepare potatoes in more tempting style than are

**Boyd Brothers'
Celebrated Revere Beach Chips.**

Dainty.   Delicious.   Always Ready to Serve.

BUY THEM OF YOUR GROCER.

Beware of imitations. The genuine Revere Beach Chips always have on the box the name and trade mark of the manufacturers.

BOYD BROS., Lynn, Mass.

W. A. IRVING,

Manufacturer of

Wood and all kinds of Fancy

Paper Boxes.

❋❋❋❋

18 Carpenter Street,

Salem, Mass.

Telephone Connection.

New England Telephone and Telegraph Company.

Connecting Principal Points in New England, Canada and States East of the Mississippi River.

Over 1500 Public Pay Stations, Indicated by Sign of the "Blue Bell" within the Company's Territory.

Do you want to avoid that business trip and thus save time and money?
Do you want to order goods and be sure of shipment to-day?
Do you want to talk with friends at home?
Do you wish, for any reason, a personal interview with parties at a distance?

Then use the "Long Distance" Telephone,
For that and that only will meet your wants.

For list of Public Pay Stations, see Official Directory, pages 26-32, Section I, and 8-19, Section II.

A circular explaining our New Measured Service Rates will be sent to you if desired.

PRIVATE LINE AND SPEAKING TUBE INSTRUMENTS.

We construct and maintain Private Lines, and lease telephones and lines to parties desiring to connect two or more places, each with the other, without passing through the Central Office Exchange. We also furnish telephones for "Speaking Tube" purposes, for use in hotels and other buildings, by which means each room may be connected with the office or janitor, and with every other room in the building. The Company will be pleased to furnish any information desired, upon application to its Executive Office,

125 MILK STREET - BOSTON, MASS.
Or by calling for Telephone, Boston, 782.

A descriptive Catalogue will be mailed to any address, upon request.

R. C. MANNING & CO.,
..COAL..

Wood and Bark. Prepared Wood and Kindlings.

289 Derby Street, Salem, Mass.
Telephone 119.

D. W. HAMILTON.　　　　　　　　　　　　　　　　J. W. BALCOMB.

Hamilton & Balcomb,
Contractors and Builders.

Planing, Sawing, Turning, Grooving.　　Pile Drivers, Wharf and Bridge Builders.
Band and Jig Sawing, Etc., Etc.

76 Lafayette Street, Salem.

Telephone 345-3.　　　　　　　　　　　　　　Mill: 279 Derby Street.

"PERFECTLY SATISFIED"

Our patrons are universally satisfied as we exercise the utmost care in furnishing the exact glasses the eyes require. We offer you fine goods, reasonable prices and, above all, satisfaction.　　EYES TESTED FREE.

REED, Optician.　243 1-2 ESSEX STREET,
Opposite Bixby's　　Up One Flight.

www.ingramcontent.com/pod-product-compliance
Lightning Source LLC
Chambersburg PA
CBHW020909230426
43666CB00008B/1374